Clarity: Beauty in Pain

Lashundra Smith

CLARITY:

Beauty in Pain

Lashundra Smith

Cover Photo Credit: Julian Smith, Jr.
Email: jsmithjrfotos@gmail.com
Instagram: Photoz_paradise

Pearly Gates Publishing LLC
INSPIRING CHRISTIAN AUTHORS TO BE AUTHORS
Pearly Gates Publishing, LLC, Houston, Texas (USA)

Clarity: Beauty in Pain

Clarity: Beauty in Pain

Copyright © 2019
Lashundra Smith

All Rights Reserved.
No portion of this publication may be reproduced, stored in any electronic system, or transmitted in any form or by any means (electronic, mechanical, photocopy, recording, or otherwise) without written permission from the publisher. Brief quotations may be used in literary reviews.

Some names and locales in the body of this work have been changed to protect the privacy of individuals.

Scripture references are taken from the New International Version of the Holy Bible and used with permission from Zondervan via Biblegateway.com
Public Domain.

ISBN 13: 978-1-947445-46-8
Library of Congress Control Number: 2018965759

For information and bulk ordering, contact:
Pearly Gates Publishing, LLC
Angela Edwards, CEO
P.O. Box 62287
Houston, TX 77205
BestSeller@PearlyGatesPublishing.com

Dedication

First and foremost, **GOD** gets all the glory for the testimonies He has given me to share with the world. I pray that through my obedience in revealing all of myself in this book that many will be healed from things that have tormented them for far too long.

To the friends and family who have supported me, encouraged me, pushed me, and ultimately forgave me: I thank you!

To my angels who went before me—**Shelia, Steve, and my parents, Sammie and Caseal Harris**: I miss you daily. I think of you in times of trouble and what you would say to me. Everything you taught me remains within and were not in vain. I am thankful that we healed from any issues before God took you home. I will never forget that you chose to love me, even though your blood did not flow through my veins. I live my life on purpose because of you.

To **Jay**: Thank you for being my rock, my best friend, my person, and an amazing father to our children. Thank you for loving me; I mean truly loving me through my grief and in times of sickness and health. You took your vows seriously, and I appreciate that more than you will ever know.

To my children—**Elexia, Kyjuan, De'Aja, and Va'Quonn**: I strive harder to be a better person because of all of you. I pray that despite being a young mom and with all my imperfections that I have given you what you need to face this world. My love for you is like an ever-flowing river: endless.

Clarity: Beauty in Pain

Table of Contents

Dedication	vi
In the Beginning	1
Truth Revealed	13
A Father's Influence	23
I Am Who God SAYS I Am	33
Journey to Independence	49
Insecurities	63
Judge Me Not	77
There is Only One God	95
Yes, Jesus Loves Me	117
My Husband:	129
Prince Charming	129
God Is a Priority,	143
Not an Option	143
Journey to Peace	161
Miracles Still Happen	173
Epilogue	181
Salvation Today	185
About the Author	186

Lashundra Smith

In the Beginning

When you are called to serve God, the enemy will send his attacks at birth. My biological mother became a teenaged mom at the age of fifteen. Her mother did not support the idea of her having a child and, instead, encouraged her to give me away. Now, many would argue that this was a good thing. After all, she was too young to raise a child—and you would be correct.

However, as that child, I didn't feel that way.

All I knew was that the person who was supposed to love me wasn't there for me. As a child, I felt she didn't love me enough to keep me and weather the storm.

This was the enemy's first attack: making me feel unloved. He knows that God is love, so if he can find a way to withhold that from the beginning, he accomplishes much.

"Whoever does not love does not know God, for God is love. This is how God showed His love among us: He sent His one and only Son into the world that we might live through Him. This is love: not that we loved God, but that He loved us and sent His Son as an atoning sacrifice for our sins. Dear friends, since God so loved us, we also ought to love one another. No one has ever seen God, but if we love one another, God lives in us, and His love is made complete in us."
(1 John 4:8-12).

For 13 years in my home, I felt unbalanced and unsure. It was as if I didn't belong, and I couldn't put my finger on why. Depression began to overwhelm me—yet another attack of the enemy. (The enemy is Satan, the one who is against anything that God creates in His image.) There were hints here and there that I was not in the right family. I had a different last name, different skin tone, and no similar familial features. My parents were not the love-you, hug-you-type; therefore, I did not feel much of an emotional attachment. It wasn't that they didn't love me; it was that they showed their affections differently. By buying things and meeting our basic needs, they felt that was enough to demonstrate love. (Unbeknownst to myself, this would later be the way I showed my affections.) As early as five years old, I can recall knowing something wasn't right. I began questioning my mother as to why my last name was different from hers. She explained it away as being her maiden name. Well, as a child, I trusted that to be true, not knowing any different.

By the age of nine, depression had consumed me. I began to express my feelings by writing poetry and songs. Around this same time, my parents stopped going to church. This was odd because they were deeply involved in the church. Therefore, I had a very short introduction to Christ. We then packed up and moved rather suddenly, prompting my whole youthful universe to be turned upside down. I was in a new environment, around unfamiliar people, and felt like an outcast. The enemy was constantly reminding me that I did not belong in this world, although God's Word says differently:

"Before I formed you in the womb, I knew you; before you were born, I set you apart: I appointed you as a prophet to the nations."
(Jeremiah 1:5)

Unfortunately, the place we moved to did not bring new friends easily. The children who lived on my street would taunt and tease me daily. I was a dark-skinned and skinny child. My parents wouldn't even allow me to dress like the other kids. I dreaded getting on the school bus each day because I knew what would be waiting for me. I tried to be unseen and unheard, hoping that if I just remained quiet, I would be invisible. It didn't work. I would often get off the bus crying. The one time I told my mom about the incessant teasing, she simply said, "Just don't worry about it," when what I needed to hear was, "You are beautiful. God made you the way He wanted and intended you to be." I needed to hear that the other kids were just jealous and on assignment from the enemy because even then, he knew what God had in store for me. I don't believe my mother purposely intended for me to feel the way I did. I believe she felt she was doing what was right by telling me to not listen to them. However, I needed to be taught my worth, to pray for myself, to pray for them, and ask God for strength to get through each day.

"Look to the LORD and His strength; seek His face always."
(1 Chronicles 16:11)

At the time, all I knew to do was fight. I was angry, sad, and lonely. I doubted myself in a way that no child should. I hated even being intelligent! Often, I tried to dumb myself down, remain quiet, and not answer any questions. The less attention, the better I could exist. The kids already teased me by calling me "Black Hawk" because of my skin tone. They then added "Nerd" to the list of names.

I began to suppress my God-given abilities. I wanted to change everything about me, including my clothes and hair. Several times, I begged my dad to take me out and get me contact lenses instead of the huge eyeglasses I was forced to wear. Now, along with "Black Hawk" and "Nerd," the kids added "Four-Eyed" to the teasing. I convinced myself that if I just changed those things about myself, I would be accepted.

I began to search for answers in man, myself, **AND** in all the wrong places. The enemy had laid his groundwork, which was the foundation that would influence my decisions for many years. He knew the promises God had for me, and he had every intention of breaking me before I received them. This is not a new trick. The Word says that there is nothing new under the sun. Take Moses, for example. Look at how the enemy tried—from the beginning—to get rid of him:

> "Then Pharaoh gave this order to all his people: 'Every boy that is born, you must throw into the Nile, but let every girl live.' Now, a man of the house of Levi married a Levite woman, and she became pregnant and gave birth to a son. When she saw that he was a fine child, she hid him for three months. But when she could hide him no longer, she got a papyrus basket for him and coated it with tar and pitch. Then, she placed the child in it and put it among the reeds along the bank of the Nile. His sister stood at a distance to see what would happen to him."
> (Exodus 1:22-2:4)

Most know how Moses' story ends. He had a purpose, and Pharaoh tried to get rid of him from the beginning—but **GOD** protected him. His mission was greater than himself. Isn't it amazing that God knows the ending to all of our stories?

I don't know how this affects you. Are you living in the past, unwilling to forgive? Or are you as a child experiencing these very feelings at this moment? Know that when you do not forgive others, it has power over you.

> "Bear with each other and forgive whatever grievances you may have against one another. Forgive as the Lord forgave you."
> (Colossians 3:13).

God gives us these guidelines in His Word to help us. Forgiving is not only the right thing to do; it also enables you to heal. God does not want this pain for you—whether you are male or female. We all deserve affection and love. It should not feel dirty, shameful, or uncomfortable. Instead, it should feel warm, understanding, and loving.

> "But you, O Lord, are a compassionate and gracious God, slow to anger, abounding in love and faithfulness."
> (Psalms 86:15).

You can decide today to stand up and get help from someone. Pray and ask God to remove you from the situation you are in while protecting you as you go through the storm. The alternative is to choose to remain in the state you are in and deal with the consequences of your decisions.

As children, most times we don't have control over what happens to us. As parents, we must intercede on our children's behalf with prayer, declaration, and by being an example. Our words will cover protect, and encourage them.

As I got older, I also realized that my biological mom was protecting me as well with her decision. She was giving me what she believed to be a better opportunity in life: a stable environment in a two-parent home. I forgave her once I acknowledged it was all a part of God's plan. Everything can have a different reaction with a different way of thinking. Is your glass half empty or half full? The fact that my birth mother gave me away was a blessing in disguise. Yes, it cost me a lot of heartache, pain, and struggle, but it also taught me strength, independence, and, above all, what not to do to my own children. God says He will give you only what you can bear. He was raising me, carrying me, and preparing me for my destiny.

If you have children (no matter the age), you have the opportunity to pray over them starting now. There are so many things they need protection over: their innocence, their hearts, and their lives. Declare that your children shall not be abused, that they shall be leaders and not followers, and that they would seek God first. Decree that the friendships and relationships they create shall come from God. Speak prosperity, good health, and that they are the head and not the tail; the leader and not the follower. Confess that they will be lenders and not borrowers, all in God's will. Teach your kids God's Word, how to praise Him, and the power of prayer in their lives at an early age. This way, even if they don't feel comfortable in coming to you, they know they can always go to God.

Most importantly, love them. Show your children love whenever possible in how you treat them and how you treat others. This lays the foundation for them to love themselves.

"Start children off in the way they should go, and even when they are old, they will not turn from it."
(Proverbs 22:6).

Put It into Practice

What areas can you improve on in raising your children? List the areas and specific scriptures to memorize so that you remain focused in those areas.

_____

_____

_____

_____

_____

_____

_____

_____

_____

_____

_____

_____

_____

_____

_____

_____

_____

Clarity: Beauty in Pain

Observe your child's behaviors and then identify the areas in which they demonstrate insecurities. Choose to encourage your child in these specific areas so they can overcome them before entering into society.

Does your child have a prayer life and consistent relationship with God? If not, what ways can you introduce this into your child's daily life?

Clarity: Beauty in Pain

Make a list of what you would like to declare and decree over your children, making a point to do this at the start of each day.

Lashundra Smith

Clarity: Beauty in Pain

Truth Revealed

"Ya still ain't told that child yet?" asked my grandmother, Madea. I overheard my grandmother fussing with my mother in hushed whispers. "Does she know Jason is her daddy?"

Confusion settled into my brain. Jason was my brother! "Surely, Madea is suffering from dementia," I thought. But then, my mind began to wander, and questions resurfaced. Why was my last name Clark and my parents' last names were Harris? I remember my mother explained it by saying I had her maiden name. Wait a minute! Her maiden name was Rhone. I was the last one born, so how was it that **ONLY** I had her maiden name? My parents had been married for over 30 years. The things I was told were not adding up!

One day, shortly after that event, I walked home from school, and I just knew. Each step I took towards my front door brought to the forefront of my mind that all the years of feeling different wasn't just my imagination. The reason my skin tone didn't match theirs. The difference in last names. The feeling of separation, even though I knew my parents loved me. It all came crashing down that they were not the family I was born into. I opened the door, determined to know the truth. I was not taking any lame excuse for an answer. I went to my mother and boldly asked, "Am I adopted?"

"What are you talking about?" she asked.

I boldy stated, "I know already. Tell me the truth."

She sat down, looking utterly defeated. She knew they couldn't lie to me any longer. She told me I was not legally adopted and that I wasn't biologically theirs, either. She went on to explain: My biological mother, Stacey, just gave me to them. She handed over her child like a doll.

Clarity: Beauty in Pain

While my mother was trying to explain, her voice faded into the background. All I could think about was that my biological mother had given me away like a mere puppy. How does someone do that? How does someone just hand over their child to people they barely know?

"How selfish, inconsiderate, and unloving," I thought.

I could only hear bits and pieces of my mother's conversation. I did manage to catch that Stacey, my birth mother, used to come to visit me for a while, but then the visits stopped. I suddenly recalled dreams I had of a woman coming to see me—dreams I hadn't spoken to my mother about until then. She just shrugged her shoulders and told me that the dreams were actually memories I had of Stacey.

Stacey met my parents through dating my older brother, Jason, whom I was raised with. My mother explained to me that they were under the impression I was their grandchild, so they took me in. Jason never denied it, so that's what they believed.

It all began making sense. The connection that my brother and I had...the extra gifts and wanting to make sure I was happy. In that brief moment, life made sense—until I approached my "brother."

Jason stated, "Your mother, Stacey, was already pregnant when I met her. I chose not to say anything because you needed a good home. I was with her during the whole pregnancy, so I, of course, grew attached to you."

Again, disappointment, hurt, and confusion sunk in. God's Word says, *"Blessed are you who hunger now, for you will be satisfied. Blessed are you who weep now, for you will laugh"* (Luke 6:21). Lord, I longed to laugh and have the worries a 13-year-old should have!

After that revelation, I became even more withdrawn. Another invisible wall went up. I was worthless and meant nothing to no one (another **LIE** the enemy put in my head). I was beginning my teen years with my hormones out of whack and my body at its most uncomfortable stages. To top it off, I was severely depressed. I just wanted to be loved. I began to search for it and hoped to find it. That love was there all along, yet I had no idea.

> **"But God demonstrates His own love for us in this: While we were still sinners, Christ died for us."**
> (Romans 5:8)

At the age of 14, I began to search for Stacey. She wasn't hard to find, as she had been living in the same home for years. Plus, my aunts still kept in touch with her. After mustering up the courage and daydreaming of how the moment would be when we met, I finally went to her home. I approached the door with an expectation of tears, joy, and apologies. Instead, all she did was open the door unsurprised. She had no look of guilt when she asked if I wanted to come in. I don't even remember her saying she was happy to see me. She didn't even attempt to hug me. She came across defensively as she said, "I did what I had to do, and I don't owe you anything."

Once again, the love I expected to receive was null and void.

Stacey did reveal that I had a brother and sister. I was the oldest of the three, and she kept in contact with them. I must admit: **THAT** hurt and brought on even more questions as to what was wrong with *ME*? Why didn't she try harder to keep up with me or see how I was doing? She gave my sister, Jaleesa, to another family but often saw her. She raised my brother, Kenneth, with my grandmother's help.

At the time, I did not know that Stacey's mother had also given **HER** away to her grandmother to raise. This confirmed the generational curse on our family. It was up to me to break that curse of having kids at a young age and then giving them away for someone else to deal with.

The enemy's hits kept coming. I couldn't breathe nor understand what I could have done to deserve all of this. God had a plan, but I was too young and unaware of what was happening. I knew He loved me and in no way wanted to harm me.

"'For I know the plans I have for you,' declares the LORD, '
plans to prosper you and not to harm you,
plans to give you hope and a future.'"
(Jeremiah 29:11).

If only I had gotten that Word put in my heart, I would have known that whatever happened and no matter how bad, God was using it to make me stronger. When we put our expectations on man, we will almost always be disappointed. Man is bound to make mistakes. As such, we cannot depend on man alone.

"God is not a man that He shall lie, nor a son of man, that He
should change His mind. Does He speak and then not act?
Does He promise and not fulfill?"
(Numbers 23:19).

God's promises are true. His Word has proven it over and over again throughout history. As for man, he has demonstrated his propensity to lie. Whether small or big lies, they are all the same. We all "fall short of the glory of God" (Romans 3:23). However, glory to God for His Word that also says "we are justified freely by His grace through the redemption that came by Christ Jesus." Although man cannot be depended upon, God still loves us and gives us grace and mercy. For us to be more like Him, we must forgive and understand that we often make a mistake in believing that man will not fail us. Once you know this, it is much easier to deal with the disappointments in life, for nothing is sure outside of God.

That day, I returned home with the experience of what happened with my mother lingering in my mind. I felt like I should just die and get it over with. Why was I here? To be unloved, sad, and lonely? It didn't seem like that's how life should be. (I wasn't aware that God makes **NO** mistakes and that *ALL* he creates has a purpose in this life.)

"Before I formed you in the womb, I knew you; before you were born, I set you apart; I appointed you as a prophet to the nations"
(Jeremiah 1:5).

Without the knowledge of just how important I am to this world, I contemplated suicide many times. I don't believe my parents had any idea of what I was feeling or that I was deeply wounded. Many times, I thought of ways that would be easiest to end my life, but I was too scared to follow through. The devil used even that to taunt me, advising me that I didn't even have the courage to end my pathetic, pitiful existence. I felt defeated, and depression continued to overwhelm me.

In this life, there is suffering, death, sickness, and struggles. Know that they are not without purpose. God promises that we will be the conquerors!

"Therefore, we do not lose heart. Though outwardly, we are wasting away, yet inwardly we are being renewed day by day. For our light and momentary troubles are achieving for us an eternal glory that far outweighs them all, So, we fix our eyes not on what is seen, but on what is unseen. For what is seen is temporary, but what is unseen is eternal."
(2 Corinthians 4:16-18).

That which I thought was the fear to end it all was God not allowing me to take my life. This life is temporary. Victory — no matter how far away — is promised to be mine...if I accept it.

"Guide me in your truth and teach me, for you are God my Savior, and my hope is in You all day long."
(Psalms 25:5)

Put It into Practice

Rejection is a part of life. Are there things you should sit down and talk to your children about, such as bullying? Discuss how important it is to understand where rejection stems from in the other person and how rejecting someone else affects that person.

_____

_____

_____

_____

_____

_____

_____

_____

_____

_____

_____

_____

_____

_____

_____

_____

Clarity: Beauty in Pain

Secrets can tear a family apart. That includes keeping secrets from your child. Although there are some things your child may not be ready to hear, there are things they should be aware of. Not talking about certain things does not make them go away. As parents, we must educate our children before the world attempts to do so in the wrong way. List some things that you know you have neglected to discuss with your child, pray about them, and then sit your child down to educate them.

_____
_____
_____
_____
_____
_____
_____
_____
_____
_____
_____
_____
_____
_____
_____
_____
_____
_____
_____

Pray and ask God to reveal to you if any behaviors show your child is withdrawn or depressed. If you identify them, list them here. Then, take the time to sit your child down and talk to them about what you have noticed and ask if there is anything wrong. Let your child talk...and you listen! This is very important in building a healthy relationship. Your child needs to feel like a person who is important, too!

_____

_____

_____

_____

_____

_____

_____

_____

_____

_____

_____

_____

_____

_____

_____

_____

_____

_____

A Father's Influence

My mother who raised me worked a lot when I was younger, so I spent a considerable amount of time with my father. I began to feel increasingly uncomfortable around him for some odd reason. I couldn't quite put my finger on the sense of unease.

One night, when my sister, Rhonda, was not home, I went snooping around the room through her stuff. I wasn't looking for anything in particular; I was just doing what little sisters do. When I reached under her bed to find a pair of cute shoes to play in, I stumbled upon a pink and white flat box. I couldn't help but be curious, so I opened it up and found within a small book. It looked like a simple, cute notebook, so I opened it up, hoping to tear out a few sheets unnoticed.

What I found shocked me!

I was only ten at the time but knew that what I was reading was not right. My sister went into details about how my father molested her night after night. She described such pain, depression, and loneliness because no one knew what she was going through. This confirmed my uneasiness with my father.

I waited some time to approach Rhonda about it, and she completely denied everything in the book. She turned her back to me and stated that she made it up just to have fun because she knew I would be snooping. My heart told me she was lying, but my head said, "That makes sense!" I dismissed the matter altogether.

I would later find out her book was **NOT** a joke.

I was a timid child and didn't know how to interact with others well because my parents were so strict. They sheltered me from many things that happened in the outside world. It was a struggle just to be in student council or even athletic activities. The other children involved in these activities had no idea what it took for me to be able to participate. The activities required afterschool practices and meetings, of which my father did not approve. He was very overprotective and claimed I shouldn't be anywhere that boys would be.

Then, the signs began to show that other things were going on in his mind. His drinking over the years had increased, and he often smelled of liquor and beer. The verbal abuse against my mother came more frequently. It hurt me to see the way he treated and talked to her at times. I would realize much later in life that he was the reason why it was hard for her to show her affections toward me. She had not been shown love herself. How could she show love towards me? She had been with my dad for all of her adult life. Therefore, she was only doing what she knew and what she had experienced. My father teased her about her weight and called her 'ignorant' on many occasions. Unbeknownst to me, the low self-esteem curse had already set up camp in our home. (When a curse begins in our families, it continues until someone stands up to break it.)

"And he passed in front of Moses, proclaiming, "The LORD, the LORD, the compassionate and gracious God, slow to anger, abounding in love and faithfulness, maintaining love to thousands, and forgiving wickedness, rebellion, and sin. Yet He does not leave the guilty unpunished; he punishes the children and their children for the sin of the fathers to the third and fourth generatlon."
(Exodus 34:6-7)

Likely happy that she didn't have to spend as much time home with my father, my mother continued to work long hours. The consequence of her actions meant that left me at home with my father, completely vulnerable. His first attempt to touch me was when he was explaining the "birds and the bees." At first, I had no idea what he was talking about, especially because he was explaining it to me in a drunken state. He called me into his bedroom and asked me to sit on the edge of the bed. He began the conversation with slurred words of what boys would do to me if I were to hang around them. I sat there shaking my head, trying to tell him I wasn't doing anything. I attempted to get up, and he pulled me back down by my arm. I was so uncomfortable. I should have known to get out of the room right then before anything happened, but I just shook the feeling off. I figured I imagined things. He then took his finger and ran it down my stomach, claiming he was demonstrating to me what boys would do. I ran out of the room, confused. I convinced myself that it wasn't a big deal, I should just ignore it, and not say anything to my mother.

A few weeks later, he called me into his room again. At the time, my nephew, Steve (who was living with us), was the only person I could talk to. I told him what had happened before and that I was scared to go in the room. We both just laughed it off and concluded there was nothing for me to worry about. So, I went into the room after he called for me a second time.

He was drunk (again) and talking about boys (again). I thought he asked me if a boy had ever tickled my breath—meaning if I had ever kissed a boy before. I shook my head no, trying to understand why he was asking me this. I was thinking I would feel better if it was my mother having this conversation with me. I smelled the alcohol on his breath as he spoke to me. Then, I stupidly asked him to repeat himself because I didn't understand. He said, "Like this," and twirled his finger around my breast. I knew this wasn't right. I knew a father shouldn't touch his daughter this way. I couldn't hide that something happened when I made it back to the room with Steve. He encouraged me to tell my mother about the incidents.

I remember the next morning seeing my mother loading up the clothes dryer. The utility room was by the master bedroom where my father was laying down. I listened intently, trying to ear-hustle in on the conversation. Although I couldn't hear what my father said, I did distinctly hear my mother. Her tone was stern but calm.

"All I have to say is if you touch her again, I will kill you!"

My dad nervously laughed it off, stating, "That girl's just lying."

I am not even sure if they knew I heard the conversation. I stood there baffled and thought, *"That's **IT**? No yelling. No screaming. No fighting? **REALLY**?"* I felt so horrible! What was I thinking? That I was that important? That she would give up all those years of marriage for me? I wasn't even their child or flesh and blood! He paid the majority of the bills and kept food on the table. I have no doubt that factored into my mother's response. Did I seriously think she would throw it all away for me? I am sure she felt that what she did was enough. She threatened him, he knew that she knew, and he wouldn't do it again. For a very long time, he avoided that close interaction with me.

I found myself making excuses for my father. He was drunk, so his judgment was impaired. I wasn't his biological daughter, so was it really considered molestation?

When I was around him, I became all the more aware of how uncomfortable I was (and still am) whenever he gets close to me. I looked at my parents' relationship and subconsciously decided it was the way relationships were supposed to be. Even if he has kids with other women while married or s creams, yells, and degrades me, it's okay because that is what my father did.

That is **NOT** what **GOD** intended love to be like.

The stereotype the world has created encourages women to believe that all the man has to do is pay the bills; other than that, he can cheat and do whatever else he so desires. Our society teaches us that women should not be respected and accept whatever a man does to them. To be a winner, you must get them first: cheat first and then just use them for their money. All along, this is never really what women want. We walk around pretending that it's enough while offering up excuses so that we can look good to others. God repeatedly shows us in His Word what love is. He specifically detailed how it should be and how it should feel in 1 Corinthians 13:4-8:

"Love is patient; love is kind. It does not envy; it does not boast, it is not proud. It is not rude; it is not self-seeking, it is not easily angered, it keeps no record of wrongs. Love does not delight in evil but rejoices with the truth. It always protects, always trusts, always hopes, and always perseveres. Love never fails."

When you study God's Word, He teaches you so much game on life! He tells you exactly what to seek in your future mate. When we ask each other how to know if a person is "the one," God has already revealed to us what will happen for us to know who "the one" is.

Not only was I young; I also wasn't up on the game. As such, I began to seek love in whatever way I could find it. I wanted and needed it desperately. It was in my face, in my words, and in my body language. I showed up in the world as, "Here I am! I will take whatever affection you have for me—as long as I can get just a *TASTE* of it!"

Clarity: Beauty in Pain

**"The Lord examines the righteous,
but the wicked and those who love violence, His soul hates."**
(Psalms 11:5)

Put It into Practice

There are some conversations that, as a parent, we wish not to have, but they are necessary in order to protect your child. Explain the do's and don'ts of another individual touching them. Show them examples of healthy touching and then explain to them when it's inappropriate. Allow your child to repeat what you said and show you what they have learned. Then, make a point to let your child know that no matter what threats the predator may say, it's imperative to let someone know so that the behavior does not continue. Write about your experience with your child.

_____

_____

_____

_____

_____

_____

_____

_____

_____

_____

_____

_____

_____

_____

Clarity: Beauty in Pain

*Ask your child this simple question: If someone hurts you, is it your fault or theirs? This is extremely important! Your child needs to know that if another person hurts them, it's **NOT** their fault and that the blame is on that other person. Record your child's response here and how you addressed it.*

_____

_____

_____

_____

_____

_____

_____

_____

_____

_____

_____

_____

_____

_____

_____

_____

_____

_____

Do you or your child understand forgiveness? If someone has hurt you or your child in the past, you both need to know the importance of forgiveness. Take time to do an in-depth study on forgiveness in the Bible. Look up scriptures that discuss forgiveness. Let them penetrate your heart and then ask God to reveal to you if there is anyone you need to forgive to move forward. Make a note of those passages of scripture here.

_____

_____

_____

_____

_____

_____

_____

_____

_____

_____

_____

_____

_____

_____

_____

_____

I Am Who God SAYS I Am

It was the summer of 1993, and I was tired of the dorky clothes, dresses down to my knees, the Jheri Curl, and being picked on. I was about to enter my freshman year of high school and refused to enter the doors the same way I left out of junior high. I began to speak my mind about what clothes I wanted to wear and cried for contact lenses the entire summer until my father gave in. I stripped my hair of that Jheri Curl, too! (Yes, I still had that style before my 9th-grade year.) I was convinced that my whole life was about to change. I thought that by changing my outward appearance, it would make me more popular. My expectations were so high, I just KNEW the guy I had been crushing on would finally take notice of me.

Imagine how I felt when those expectations tumbled down. I entered high school and realized **NOTHING** had changed. People still saw me as the same quiet, nerdy Shunda.

I suppressed my personality to keep from making a fool of myself, always thinking, "What if I say the wrong thing?" I had a very small group of friends and thought I had finally found a great friend in Tamika. We grew extremely close. Our parents were relatives through marriage, so we considered ourselves cousins. She was one of the few people my parents let me spend time with. I shared a lot with her—a little too much, which would, in the end, terminate our friendship.

Eventually, I took my eyes off the guy I was crushing on, realizing that I wasn't ever going to be popular enough for him and decided, instead, to focus on who *WAS* paying attention to me. Taurus Davis was my first boyfriend. He wasn't really my type; he was way too tall for me, and his nose was so big, I was afraid it would hit me when we kissed. Even though I wasn't greatly interested in him, I figured what the heck! I was tired of being a loner. I wanted to fit in! So, Taurus and I began to talk on the phone and got to know each other. Guess what happened? I started to really like him! I was extremely shy, so most times, I had Tamiko either on the phone with us or in our presence.

Our daily phone calls got to where we couldn't have them unless all three of us were on the line. It seemed so innocent, I didn't think much about it. I trusted both of them, and we were always on the phone together, so I felt it was okay. Little did I know they had begun conversations of their own when we hung up from our calls.

Taurus was the first guy I ever kissed. It was extremely uncomfortable, awfully wet, and yes, that nose of his was in the way. Still, I was dedicated to him. I believed this was just the beginning and that it would only get better. I wanted to be in love, no matter how uncomfortable it made me.

In an instant, it all changed with a basketball game.

The Monday morning after our Friday night basketball game, I returned to school to stares and whispers. It was beyond the usual paranoid thinking that people were talking about me. They were actually staring, pointing, and whispering every time I walked by.

Living in a small town does not allow for many secrets. Nothing was sacred. If you didn't want anyone to know something, then you had to take it to your grave.

Finally, a friend who I still cherish until this moment, Denise, told me what all the commotion was about. Taurus had cheated on me with Tamika in front of the basketball team, right before Friday night's game. They had sex on the couch in front of people! My friend—the one I had sat on the phone with for **HOURS**, giggling and talking about Taurus—went behind my back and had sex with my first and only boyfriend!

I was left devastated…again. Unloved…again. And questioning myself…*AGAIN*!

I got rid of both my so-called friend and him and decided it was best to move on quickly. Instead of closing up, this incident left my heart wide open for more pain. I am sure the next man I was to meet saw me coming from a mile away.

It took some time, but I finally convinced my parents to let me spend the night sometimes with my friend Chantel. She was the only one who accepted me as I was and remained cool with me, although my parents were super strict. When I would go to Chantel's house, that was the only time I could let loose. We often walked to the park on Sundays and enjoyed what little freedom I had. One of the times I spent the night, we ended up at a party at one of the small clubs in town. I remember feeling so out of place. I never danced in front of anyone and couldn't remember when I had been around so many people all at once. I am sure my insecurities came shining through as I swayed back and forth on the dance floor.

That's when I met Damion.

Damion was a 21-year-old man. I was only 15 years old at the time. I wasn't prepared for the game he was about to run on me. I was naïve, disillusioned, and desperate for attention. I was basically right where he needed me to be. He told me how beautiful my eyes were, which is something most everyone else talked about negatively as they constantly pointed out how big they were. And the same body everyone joked about being so skinny, he complimented by telling me how flat my stomach was and how good my legs looked. He pretended to understand how strict my parents were and used it to his advantage to convince me he would do anything to be with me. I would often tell my parents I was staying with Chantel when I was actually going to spend the night with Damion.

He would sometimes sneak into my house while my parents were asleep and just sit and talk with me. We would play games, and he would listen attentively to the poetry I wrote for him. Damion paid attention to and spent time with me, which was what I so desperately needed. I truly believed he loved me, and I wanted to show him that I loved him. He was a man who expected grownup things. I believed I was his girlfriend through and through, so it was time to act like it.

My first time having sex was on the side of my house in the wet grass on a blanket. He acted like having sex under the stars was so romantic. How foolish of me to believe him!

Not even six weeks later, I remember the sickness that overcame me. It was a just-not-feeling-right moment and knew that something was wrong. My sister, Yolanda, took me to the clinic and, of course, I was pregnant. I only had sex one time, and I was **PREGNANT**! I couldn't believe my luck. This horrible life was never-ending! The turns my stomach was doing was in no way comparable to what I thought my mother would do when she found out. The drive home from the clinic was the worst feeling ever. I was so scared, I ended up telling my mother while outside and behind the car so that she wouldn't hit me. She was left speechless and walked back into the house with hurt and disappointment written all over her face. That silence hurt more than what I **THOUGHT** she would do. She was disappointed in me. Not only that, she was sad for me. She knew how it would profoundly affect my future.

My mother and I began to butt heads about my "situation." She didn't want Damion involved with my son at all. She was angry at him for being so much older and taking advantage of me. I kept trying to explain I knew what I was doing and that it was unfair to punish the baby. She didn't care. She couldn't see past her rage. Damion even tried to come by to introduce himself and explain he would be there for the baby. My mother screamed at and threatened him to get him out of the house. I was fearful of even speaking to him at this point. When I did get up the courage to mention how I felt, my mother grabbed me the neck and began to choke me! My heart ached because she was so angry with me.

Damion, of course, didn't live up to the expectations I had for him. After I became pregnant and the whole town whispered behind my back, someone finally gave me the bad news: Damion had a girlfriend he had been with since high school. When I approached him about it, he made it clear she was the priority and wasn't going anywhere.

I had given up my virginity and defiled my temple for a man who had no further use for me.

> "Do you not know that your bodies are members of Christ Himself? Shall I then take the members of Christ and unite them with a prostitute? Never! Do you not know that he who unites himself with a prostitute is one with her in body? For it is said, 'The two will become one flesh.' But he who unites himself with the Lord is one with Him in Spirit. Flee from sexual immorality. All other sins a man commits are outside his body, but he who sins sexually sins against his own body. Do you not know that your body is a temple of the Holy Spirit, who is in you, whom you have received from God? You are not your own; you were bought at a price. Therefore, honor God with your body."
> (1 Corinthians 6:15-20)

Wow! That scripture speaks volumes! God uses prostitutes as an example, but this refers to anyone you have sex with outside of marriage. You become one flesh. That is why it is so hard to let go of someone once you have sex with them — because you become one. This is why God designed sex for marriage, so that you may become one with your spouse. That connection (which is so strong) is meant to keep marriages together. It is also the obvious reason why you shouldn't deny your spouse sex, so as to keep you connected to one another (1 Corinthians 7:3-5).

I had completely dishonored God and myself. As it is, most actions come with consequences…oftentimes, not the best ones. Even then, God can make those consequences work out for our good — if we allow Him to.

I was 15 years old and, after one wrong action…one lousy decision, I was about to be a mother. I hadn't paid much attention in sex education class, and the subject was taboo in my household. The only conversation we had was simply, "You better **NOT** have sex!" I had just started kissing and had no idea I would move that fast! I was confused and couldn't believe what was happening to me. I was about to have a baby — and I was a baby! The father wasn't trying to be with me, and his girlfriend was telling me the best thing to do was get an abortion. My brother, Jason, even said I needed to think about my education and get rid of the child.

All the while, I was reminded: I was walking in similar shoes as my birth mother.

I couldn't get the abortion. All I could think about was the fact that my mother had given me away. How could I, in my right mind, do that to my own child? Not just give him away, but take his life! My parents and Damion's girlfriend told me not to speak to him anymore. Everyone expected so much of me.

Stop talking to my child's father.

Get rid of the baby.

Move on with my life accordingly.

I couldn't believe Damion didn't care about me. How could someone spend time with me the way he did, take something so precious (my virginity), and then just **LEAVE**? It began to register with me that this was just how men are. Accept it, take the little bit of attention I can get, and move on. I didn't know my worth. I didn't know **GOD'S** worth for me.

"For You created my inmost being; You knit me together in my mother's womb. I praise You because I am fearfully and wonderfully made; Your works are wonderful, I know that full well. My frame was not hidden from You when I was made in the secret place. When I was woven together in the depths of the earth, Your eyes saw my unformed body. All the days ordained for me were written in Your book before one of them came to be."
(Psalms 139:14-17).

God advises us that we are worth so much more than we allow ourselves to be treated and that He took great effort in creating every one of us.

"And even the very hairs of your head are all numbered."
(Matthew 10:30)

After much thought and pillow-soaked tears, I decided to keep my son. No matter what anyone said, I knew I could not abort my unborn child. I was a sophomore in high school and, after looking back at my situation, I believe God was preparing me for my son's birth all along. For some odd reason, I was extremely interested in chromosomes in biology class. I asked more questions than usual and took a particular interest in all the teacher had to say about it. I paid especially close attention to the topic of Down-Syndrome children.

My son was born at Parkland Memorial Hospital in Dallas, Texas. I was in labor for 22 hours and determined not to scream for fear of what the nurses would say to me. I already knew what they were thinking by the obvious we-do-not-approve stares. After my son, VaQuonn, was born, the doctors came to me with some surprising news. I remember them trying to tell me in a calm, matter-of-fact way that my son was "different." They told me that sometimes, despite the prenatal care and sonograms, unforeseen things happen during a pregnancy.

"Do not be alarmed, Shunda. Your son has Down Syndrome."

My son was mentally disabled and had a hole in his heart they would soon have to repair so that he could live. Tears streamed down my face. How was I supposed to be **CALM**? This doctor had no idea what I had already gone through for the last 16 years!

I kept asking myself, "What did I do to deserve this?" I was not the first teenager to ever have a baby, so why did this happen to me? I felt like the whole world was against me and that this was just my punishment for being me.

I recalled all I had learned in class and knew the teacher had said this most often happened with older women. I was sixteen! A freaking sophomore in **HIGH SCHOOL**! I now realize God was preparing me for this life in that class. My son would be the reason why I took such special interest and asked so many questions. Although I was upset and angry, I knew what my son was going through.

I began to think that maybe I should have had the abortion. Was this my punishment for not listening to everyone? Now, my son would have to suffer the same — if not worse — cruelties this world has to offer. I was ashamed and didn't even want to utter the words "mental retardation." I **HATED** those words. I **HATED** to hear them spoken or joked about. I hesitated to tell his father what the doctors said, but when Damion came to see him at the hospital, he accepted our son right on the spot. He showed no fear of his circumstances and assured me our son would be much smarter than the doctors said he would be. Those words helped, but they didn't take the pain away — especially when I knew I would be the one raising him.

When I returned to school to show pictures of my son, I hoped that no one would notice his widespread eyes and protruding tongue. Unfortunately, they were not missed. I recall a girl from school asking to see a picture of him, as I could hear the snickers and giggling coming from behind me. I thought it was nothing until I later found my son's picture crumpled up on top of the trashcan in the ladies' bathroom. That girl had only asked for the photo to make fun of him because she had already heard the talk about him. Once again, the world was as cruel as I thought it would be. The world didn't disappoint! But our Heavenly Father smiles down on us, no matter the circumstances.

> **"As a father has compassion on his children,
> so the LORD has compassion on His children."**
> (Psalms 103:13)

Soon enough, I would realize how ignorant my view of my son was, along with the world's. God makes no mistakes, and my son is more blessed than most because he doesn't have to worry about the troubles of this world. He has joy when we feel sadness. He has love when we only feel anger. He enjoys the smallest things that we take for granted.

When my son turned eight months old, I noticed he had very little energy. He wasn't able to keep any of his food down, nor was he gaining any weight. The doctors said it was time for him to have the open-heart surgery. I was sixteen and not only was I dealing with the fact that I was a mother, but the mother to a special-needs child with a congenital disability. I was overwhelmed and needed guidance.

While some of my family members and I were in the Intensive Care waiting area during the surgery, I met a young man's mother, Teresa, whose son was also there due to an unfortunate accident at Wetting Wild Water Park. He almost drowned and was on life support. Suddenly, my worries seemed insignificant. However, the conversation I was about to have with her would change my way of thinking in regards to my son for the rest of my life. God was revealing Himself to me through others, giving me a taste here and there of His love for me.

Teresa explained to me that her son also had Down Syndrome. She walked me to his room and showed me the pictures of all their family. I could see how much they loved him. This woman was the stepmother of a famous rapper, Tupac, yet she was so humble. I couldn't believe she was even taking the time out to speak with me. She told me with great assurance that God chose me to take care of such a special gift because He trusted me. He knew my heart enough to know I would take care of my son to the best of my ability and give him the love I felt he deserved. Teresa told me that I should hold my head up proudly, knowing that God believed in me that much at such a young age. God made me stronger than I gave myself credit for. He was with me through it all. God trusted me to give my son the love I felt I had yet to receive. I was to give my son unconditional love and, in return, I would receive that same love from him.

> **"Charm is deceptive, and beauty is fleeting;
> but a woman who fears the Lord is to be praised."**
> (Proverbs 31:30).

Put It into Practice

You are beautiful in God's eyes! Write down your best attributes and focus on them daily, instead of focusing on your flaws.

_____
_____
_____
_____
_____
_____
_____
_____
_____
_____
_____
_____
_____
_____
_____
_____
_____
_____
_____

Clarity: Beauty in Pain

How important is your body? Does your body belong to you or God? Explain your "why."

When you are unable to respect yourself, how can others? List ways you have noticed you allow others to disrespect you. What will you do about this moving forward?

Do you agree that it's important to wait for marriage to have sex? Why or why not?

Lashundra Smith

Journey to Independence

After returning home with my son, I thought that somehow things at home would change. For some crazy reason, I believed I was grown now and wouldn't have to live by my parents' strict rules. I had a child of my own, so how could they possibly tell **ME** what to do? Well, I was in for an unpleasant surprise because not a single thing changed. I was still bound to the house like a cellmate. I felt like all my room needed was some bars and a guard standing at the entrance.

I couldn't endure it any longer. I had to go. The uneasiness between my father and I, along with the unbendable rules made me feel like was literally going to go insane! I asked Stacey if I could stay with her, emphasizing what my father did to convince her to say yes. Otherwise, she didn't seem too excited about me staying, but she cared enough not to leave me in that situation. I am aware that my choice hurt my mother. She appeared angry, sad, and disappointed all at the same time. I don't believe I fully understood what I was doing to her. She chose to raise me, and I was leaving. I couldn't let go of the fact that my father was still there. I was torn in my decision but felt it was the best thing for me to do at the time. As a matter of fact, my mother was so angry, she refused to allow me to bring my son with me! (I believe it was also because she knew what I was leaving to deal with.) I was allowed to get my son only on the weekends, while she kept and cared for him during the week.

Getting to know my biological mother was not what I thought it would be. My fantasy of us living together was rudely interrupted the moment I stepped into her home. My brother, Kenneth, was spoiled and got into trouble all the time, and Stacey apparently did not know what discipline was. She would threaten him constantly with punishment and then turn around and let him do whatever he wanted to do from the start. I went from total domination to no rules at all.

Clarity: Beauty in Pain

In stark contrast, my mother back at home was very responsible. The bills were paid, groceries were bought, and the food was cooked. I was in a whole other territory with Stacey. We were pretty much responsible for feeding ourselves unless Dan, my stepfather, did the cooking. We hardly had any money to do anything, and we slept on mattresses on the floor. Stacey was constantly at Bingo, losing the little money we had — and expecting US to pick up the slack. (I would soon find out she had many other "habits" that caused her to be the way she was.)

I was receiving a disability check for my son that was supposed to be used to help with raising him. I honestly tried to do so, but Stacey always had her hand out for it. I wasn't permitted to cash the check on my own. She used the fact that I was a minor without identification as an excuse to take me to cash it instead of taking me to get identification. No sooner than the check was cashed would she start saying, "We have no food, and I don't know how we are going to pay the bills…" She put all the responsibilities of an adult on me! They were things that had to be paid for before I moved in with her and should **NOT** have been my responsibility at the age of sixteen.

Each month, the financial situation grew progressively worse. I was hardly able to send my mother any money for the care of my son. Stacey was so manipulative, to the point I felt like if I didn't give her the money, I would be put out. Whenever I told her no, she became extremely upset about it.

I distinctly remember receiving my check one month and being determined not to give her any money. I needed to send my mother money to get baby food for my son. After all, it wasn't her responsibility to do that, and I wasn't there. It was the least I could do. In response, Stacey went on and on saying, "We have no food in this house. That money is just as much yours as it is your son's. I promise to give it back to you in time for you to send it to him."

I stressed to her, "I have to send the money now. My mom barely has any, and I have to make sure my son gets **HIS** food." I conceded and gave her the money. She promised me that she would return it and, of course, it never happened. Again, I put my trust in the wrong thing: man!

"God is not a man, that He should like, nor a son of man, that He should change His mind. Does He speak and then not act? Does He promise and not fulfill?"
(Numbers 23:19)

God even takes it a step further and tells us:

"Stop trusting in man, who has but a breath in his nostrils. Of what account is he?"
(Isaiah 2:22).

God makes it so clear, straightforward, and simple. If we only paid attention to His Word, what a wealth of knowledge we would gain.

The living situation was not working for me. I had to make a decision: Do I go back home and deal with my dad or stay with Stacey and miss out on my son's life while she continued to take all **HIS** money? It was a difficult decision to make. I had just met my sister, Jaleesa, and grown so attached to her. I felt like I finally had a true friend. She had even decided to go to high school with me, even though she lived in another school district. Still, I was missing my son, my old friends, and the fact that my parents let me be a child and took care of me.

In the end, I packed up and moved back home with my parents. I figured things couldn't be the same. I had been gone

Clarity: Beauty in Pain

for a while and felt my dad wouldn't do what he did to me again. I was wrong.

I was now of driving age and ready for a car. My dad took me to his dealership where I chose a nice, red convertible Volkswagen. I was so excited, I completely forgot about the nervousness I felt when he and I were together all alone. A few weeks later, we went to the store in my new car. On the way home, he began to talk about when you receive something, you should give something back. I admit: I was a bit confused by what he meant and looked at him strangely because I had no idea where the conversation was going. He saw the look on my face, and I assume he felt that was a sign for him to show me what he meant. He reached his hand down in between my legs. I jumped, causing him to jerk his hand back. I was so startled at what he just did, so I didn't respond whatsoever…and neither did he.

To rewind my story a bit: A few weeks prior to that unwanted hand incident, I had gotten into trouble for using the car to go farther than Terrell (the city we lived in). I drove to Dallas to see a boy and got lost coming back. On top of being lost, the motor blew out in the car, and I got stuck on the side of the road. I had to walk ten miles or more to find a phone. All the while as I was walking, I thought, "Lord, I can't do **ANYTHING** without getting caught!" My father came to get me. He was silent and visibly upset.

With all that just happened, I was hesitant to say something to my mother about the recent hand between my legs event. I had a strong feeling that my dad would say I was making it all up because I was tired of their strict rules. I left the house that day with every intention on not returning, but I had nowhere to go. I didn't want to be in that home anymore. Of course, when I decided to tell my mother what happened, my father did just as I thought he would and blamed it on me not wanting to follow the rules. There was so much doubt, fear, and confusion clouding my brain. I didn't even know right from wrong anymore. My next steps were uncertain.

> **"For God is not a God of disorder, but of peace.
> As in all the congregations of the saints."**
> (1 Corinthians 14:33)

I should have just sat still, prayed over the situation, waited for an answer from God, or even allowed Him to repair the situation in my home. I figured I would be better off going back to stay with Stacey and deal with the money issue rather than deal with my father.

Against my better judgment, I moved back in with Stacey. I was just beginning my junior year of high school and carrying the burdens of an adult. At this tumultuous time in my life, I didn't know I could pray and cast all my worries on God. His Word can be such a comfort to us.

In the Book of Peter, He tells us, "Cast all your anxiety on Him because He cares for you" (1 Peter 5:7).

I had to leave my son again because I knew it was best for both of us. I made a promise that I would get him back as soon as I graduated high school. I also decided it was best not to transfer his disability checks to me. My mother was the one providing for him, so she was entitled to receive that money. She was still doing the best she could to help me, even though I was leaving her. I knew that she would protect him and not let anything happen to him.

Meanwhile, Stacey was upset that I was allowing his checks to remain going to my parents' house. She reminded me of this daily. Again, I felt unloved, unwanted, and unnecessary.

During my senior year, Jaleesa and I were at the mall when I set my sights on this guy walking with his friends. We met and exchanged numbers. He went to another school, so most of our conversation was on the phone. I really liked him and wanted to keep him. When he came to visit me, we had sex. It was actually pretty awful sex. I was inexperienced, and he was well-endowed. It was horribly uncomfortable, so less than five minutes later, I told him to get up. Needless to say, he was upset with me and started acting like he didn't even know me.

Oh. And I was pregnant again. I hadn't even enjoyed the act of sex to its fullest, yet there I was about to be a mother to **TWO** kids! I decided to get an abortion. It seemed to be the best option. I could not have another child. Admittedly, I was also fearful of having another special-needs child. The doctors were unable to explain how it happened before, and I was scared of my luck. I needed to finish school and take care of the child I already had. I didn't know how I was going to get the money for the abortion, working for minimum wage at Kentucky Fried Chicken. I was scared out of my mind and looked for an easy way out, even if it meant killing my own child. God's Word clearly says in Exodus, "Thou shall not murder." I, however, didn't think it was a big deal. After all, others have done it, so what will be *SO* wrong if I did? I made a mistake by having unprotected sex and figured an abortion was the best way to deal with the unplanned pregnancy.

God had something else in mind…

As life would have it, I met another guy named Fred. We were hitting it off great, but I had yet to tell him I was pregnant. We were still in the talk-on-the-phone-until-you fall asleep phase because we had only been dating a few weeks. Still, I knew he cared about me in that short amount of time. When I finally got up the nerve to tell him I was pregnant, his initial response was just as I expected: "I can't deal with this right now. I don't think it's going to work," and he hung up the phone. I wasn't surprised; hurt, but definitely not surprised. I cried myself to sleep that night with a great determination to get rid of the baby and start over.

The next morning, Fred called me back and told me he didn't want to be without me. I couldn't believe it! He was choosing to be there for me, pregnant and all!

Time seemed to fly by. Before I knew it, I was three months pregnant and still trying to come up with the money for the abortion when the doctor called about the results of my sonogram. My sister, Jaleesa, was there and before I could deny wanting to know what gender the baby was, she grabbed the phone. When she hung up, she had this big, stupid grin on her face and blurted out, **"IT'S A GIRL! AND SHE'S HEALTHY!"** She knew that was going to change my mind about getting the abortion. I was carrying a healthy baby girl. How could I abort her?

I decided to keep and love her! I felt I was starting over. I had a boyfriend who liked me for me, and I was having a baby girl.

Our senior year flew by fast. Fred was doing great in school and was very good at football. I knew he wanted to go away to college, and I was scared of losing him. I began to say stuff to him suggesting that when he left, he would probably find a girlfriend without kids and that there would be too much temptation for him to pass up. I argued with him about how long-distance relationships never worked. I was insecure, scared, and trying to push him to do what I thought he was going to do anyway: break up with me. It got to where we couldn't talk about anything else. He finally gave in and broke up with me. I truly regretted it once it actually happened. What I did know for a fact was that if it were meant to be, we would have remained in a relationship. He would have fought for me to make it work. Oh well. I was too young to appreciate a real relationship anyway.

Meanwhile, back at home, Stacey was divorcing my stepdad, Chris. They argued all the time and, at one point, he tried to hit her. One thing I will say for her is she wasn't about to stand for that, so he was **OUT**! However, her decision affected me, and I had to stay with my grandmother while she got herself together. I couldn't have been more depressed. I was living with my grandmother, who acted as if she didn't even want me there. She was the same woman who told my mother just to give me away. She favored my younger brother and gave him money for food, leaving me to fend for myself.

When I was six months pregnant, I had to catch two buses across town for school and then go into work. When I would get paid, Stacey would come over and beg all my money right out of my hands. I couldn't take it anymore, but I couldn't go back home to my dad, and I couldn't stay with Stacey, either. It was time to leave granny's house. Jaleesa's sister she was raised with, Antoinette, took me in. I should have seen the confusion coming a mile away. Antoinette was bossy, loud, and sarcastic. I already had a full plate; now I had to deal with her.

Antoinette was a hard sleeper. She slept so hard that most times when I got off work, it took forever for me to get in the house. Nothing seemed to be enough for her. It didn't matter whether or not I did the chores. She always seemed to have something negative to say. One night, when I got off work after catching a bus from downtown Dallas to Pleasant Grove, I returned home to find Antoinette not answering the door again. I knocked on the door for **HOURS**. She finally opened the door at three in the morning.

If it wasn't one thing, it was another. I couldn't do this every day; go to school, go to work, and then beat on the door until only Lord knows what time to finally go to sleep. I was going to have to move again! I began to talk back with my mother in Terrell. My sister, Sheila, decided it would be best that I stay with her. Ahh! **FINALLY!** A sane situation! I had peace. I knew I couldn't stay there forever, but at least no one was taking my money, abusing me, or not letting me in the house. I was also able to see my son again since my sister was the one keeping him while my mother went to work. It seemed as though my life was about to have some order.

Senior prom was approaching, and I was pregnant with no date. I settled for my soon-to-be daughter's dad, Jonathan, to go with me. We got a hotel room and had the most uncomfortable sex again. This time, I didn't even allow him to finish. I laid there that night thinking about how stupid I was to have sex with him when I had dated Fred for months and never did anything with him. I was completely backward! I had convinced myself that Jonathan and I were about to have a child, so that's who I should be having sex with. I assumed now that I was having the baby and had broken up with Fred, Jonathan and I could begin a relationship for our baby girl.

I assumed wrong. He was not interested.

It didn't surprise me. I was so used to this outcome, I don't think I even got upset about it. I just moved on.

By God's grace alone, I graduated high school with honors. I walked across the stage proudly—big belly and all. I was still at my job as a Customer Service Representative for Greyhound Lines and was able to afford my own place. On graduation night, instead of celebrating with everyone else, I was moving into my own apartment. Finally, I could breathe a little.

Clarity: Beauty in Pain

The curse on my family of not raising our own children was broken because I finally had both of my kids with me. Still, I was missing something. I felt like I needed a man to define me because I had yet to deal with the pain of all that happened. I chose to, instead, file it all away in the back of my subconscious and continue to live my life the only way I knew how.

"And the God of all grace, who called you to His eternal glory in Christ, after you have suffered a little while, will Himself restore you and make you strong, firm, and steadfast."
(1 Peter 5:7).

Put It into Practice

How important is it for you to show your child stability? In what ways do you feel you do this?

_____

_____

_____

_____

_____

_____

_____

_____

_____

_____

_____

_____

_____

_____

_____

_____

Clarity: Beauty in Pain

Are there some past pains you need to let go of? List them here and ask God to take them away so that you can move forward.

_____

_____

_____

_____

_____

_____

_____

_____

_____

_____

_____

_____

_____

_____

_____

_____

_____

_____

_____

_____

_____

_____

What things do you always worry about? List those things, pray here, and focus on ways to release those worries to God once and for all.

_____
_____
_____
_____
_____
_____
_____
_____
_____
_____
_____
_____
_____
_____
_____
_____
_____
_____
_____
_____

Insecurities

After moving into my own home, my sister, Jaleesa, and her cousin, Teisha, often spent weekends with me. We were getting to know each other and realized we all loved to sing—one of the main things we had in common (besides our goofiness). We had big dreams of becoming a singing group, calling ourselves "Exquisite." We practiced all the time, with me being tasked to write the songs and even create dance steps. I was beginning to think that was the reason for all the pain I endured: to help me write songs with meaning. I poured my heart into writing and expressing myself through the lyrics. I was genuinely hopeful that someday, all the pain I experienced would not have been in vain.

The three of us were so involved in the group, people would find us singing anywhere, at any time. Several times, we came in contact with possible opportunities to make it in the entertainment industry, but nothing ever came to fruition. Even so, we created a bond I believed could not be broken. We shopped, got our hair done, and partied together. I felt I **FINALLY** found real friendship.

That was until men got involved.

I met Torey, and it felt like fate. I had a secret crush on him during high school but never acted on it. One day, while at the grocery store, we spotted each other and, soon after, began to spend a lot of time together. (I can easily recall how cute he was!) I was superficial and blinded by his good looks. I couldn't see past his ignorance. He would get upset and talk crazy to my sister, and I would just laugh it off. I didn't realize how much it bothered her until one day, she got so upset with me and said, "Either you say something to him about it, or I'm not coming over here anymore!" I did speak to him, but he continued to say rude things to her now and then.

I still didn't get rid of him, though.

At one point, he got so bold that when Jonathan called me to discuss his daughter, Torey grabbed the phone and told him he couldn't come over anymore. Jonathan had been inconsistent with her car, so I thought Torey was a good man by telling him just to stay away. Well, Jonathan thought otherwise.

He showed up at my apartment and kicked the door in. I ran to the back of the room and grabbed my baby to protect her from what I was sure was going to be a ferocious beatdown in the confines of my living room—only to notice that Torey was cowered in the corner. I was in **SHOCK**! He talked all this mess and acted so macho, and he was cowering in the corner! I was completely turned off by that sight. He had to go! Not long after that day, I broke up with him.

Some time passed, and I met Jaelon. He wasn't like any of the other guys I dealt with. He was genuine, honest, and cared for me. I was *SO* not prepared for him. When we began to date, I figured he would be just like the rest of them, so I continued to date other guys in hopes of not getting my heart broken. I cheated on Jaelon with another guy and felt so guilty about it that I told on myself! He was very angry with me. I remember realizing at that moment: **THIS MAN REALLY CARES FOR ME!** I begged him not to break up with me, explaining I knew I made a mistake. I shared with him my history of relationships with men and how I struggled with trust.

That was the first time I ever openly expressed my truth.

Jaelon forgave me. I mean **TRUE** forgiveness, never bringing up what happened again. Despite what I had done, he didn't retaliate by cheating on me. For the first time, I felt genuine love from a man. He constantly told me how beautiful I was and reminded me daily of how special I was to him. We spent quality time together (meaning our relationship's foundation wasn't built on sex). Everything he had, he shared with me. I drove his car, and he even watched the kids when I wanted to go out with friends. The bonus here was that he loved my kids! His mom adored me and would often take me shopping and spend time with me. His father was a minister and had raised him with a lot of values.

Well, as **MY** life would have it, the insecurities I had yet to deal with officially came creeping back in. I began to question why he was with me. I had kids, I cheated on him, and I wasn't all that pretty (at least according to my previous relationships). No matter how much he showed me differently, I refused to allow him all the way in. I constantly interjected negative comments about myself whenever he said something positive. I pushed and pushed until he finally caved in and broke it off. He vehemently told me, "You don't love yourself. I cannot convince you of my love for you anymore. I can't love you like I want until you love yourself."

I was devastated! I felt like someone close to me had died. I kept calling and telling him I could get it right and that I would no longer bring up the negatives about myself. It was too late, though. He had already moved on.

I felt like an idiot as the memories played back in my mind of all the precious moments Jaelon and I shared. There were many moments full of love that I missed so much. I let the devil convince me once more that I was tainted and unworthy. I distinctly remember the enemy repeating, "He doesn't want you. You don't actually believe that **YOU**—who has kids and is skinny and ugly like they say—have someone who loves you?" I believed what the enemy said about me so much, I convinced others to accept it as well. I allowed all my past experiences to interrupt the present, instead of loving myself or recognizing that God loved me. I assumed God didn't want to have anything to do with me either. How could He, after all the things I had done?

> "Who shall separate us from the love of Christ?
> **Shall trouble or hardship or persecution or famine or nakedness or danger or sword? As it is written for your sake, we face death all day long: we are considered as His sheep to be slaughtered. No, in all these things we are more than conquerors through Him who loved us. For I am convinced that neither death nor life, neither angels nor demons, neither the present nor the future, nor any powers, neither height nor depth, nor anything else in all creation, will be able to separate us from the love of God that is in Christ Jesus our Lord."**
> (Romans 8:35-39).

God loves us and wants the best for us, no matter what we have done. He can still bless us, even when we aren't worthy of His blessings and too foolish to realize He exists. He tells us that nothing—not **ONE** thing—can separate us from His love. The enemy knew I had no idea of Christ's love for me; therefore, I did not know how to love myself, let alone let someone else love me.

It's natural to want, desired, and need love, but nothing can come in until we rid ourselves of the trash that dwells in our hearts. If I couldn't love myself or appreciate being alone with myself, how could I expect someone else to love me? When we take time to love ourselves, it makes us better for the next person. It allows us to find out what it is we really want instead of accepting whatever comes our way. Loving ourselves also reminds us that we deserve what is best for ourselves and should accept nothing less.

One day, after the breakup with Jaelon, I ended up getting a terrible toothache (as if the depression I felt wasn't enough). Jaleesa was over, so I took a pain pill and fell asleep, sure that my sister would keep a watchful eye on the kids. When I awoke, my front door was open, and my kids were gone. I was in a state of panic and ran out the door looking for them. At first, I assumed my sister had them, but then I remembered her saying to me that she was leaving. I was deep into my sleep, so I thought I was dreaming. I ran to the front office thinking someone snatched my kids, and the police were there. My kids were in the back of a squad car and being taken away to Child Protective Services. I thought my life was indeed going to end if I lost my kids. That night, I wanted to die. I wanted to end it all, but God protected me and, after my sister explained to the authorities that I was truly asleep and on sedatives, they released my children back to me the following day.

Remember I stated there are consequences for our actions? Well, with all the drama that happened while living in my apartment (Jonathan kicking in the door and the police coming about the kids), my landlord wouldn't allow me to renew my lease. I was okay with moving out, especially since there were so many bad memories attached to that space. Unfortunately, since they did not tell me I had to move until my lease was up, I was forced to move back in with my parents again! After several dreadful months, I ended up on Section 8 housing assistance and moved into another apartment.

I was so depressed about the breakup with Jaelon, I cried for months. I played Brandy's "Never Say Never" compact disc until it scratched and would no longer play. It seemed like she was in my heart with those songs. I wanted to stay visiting my pity party and never come back out to play. I wanted Jaelon back! I felt there was no way God was going to bless me with love like that again. I messed up. That was it, and there was no going back.

Another trick of the enemy is that replay button he loves to tap. The devil pushes that repeat button in our minds repeatedly, so that we can stay in that wretched place. He does that to remind us of our failures and to discourage us from getting up and trying life again.

Once again, I began to focus on material things. I wanted to look my best at all times for the wrong reasons. Nothing I did was for me; it was for everyone else's reaction. I couldn't focus if I didn't have my money right or wasn't the sharpest thing walking.

"Keep your lives free from the love of money and be contents with what you have, because God has said,
"Never will I leave you; never will I forsake you.'"
(Hebrews 13:5).

In my materialistic state, I bought a car and began fixing it up. I purchased expensive rims and even went so far as to get a sound system installed. I went to the bizarre and bought all the necessary items: speakers, new compact disc player, and an amplifier. I told a few friends I believed I could trust about my purchases and before I was able to put the sound system in, it was all stolen out of the trunk of my car. I honestly remember thinking, "Shunda, you seriously have the worst luck in the world!"

I knew one of my friends betrayed me because no one else knew I had bought the stuff except them. How do items recently bought disappear on the **SAME DAY** of purchase from the trunk of a locked car without obvious signs of a break-in? Of course, no one would own up to the theft, but I knew that only those who had access to my keys could have done something like this. I felt so violated and stupid again!

But this was in no comparison to what was coming next...

I decided to have a small get-together in my apartment with some friends. While we danced, mingled, and ate, a few of the boys who lived in the complex decided to take my car keys and steal my car! After the party was over, I walked outside and noticed my car was **GONE**! I had no insurance, so there wasn't much I could do about it. I did, however, call the police. They found the car several days later completely gutted out and torn apart. It was no longer drivable. Once again, I had no transportation and was back to using the bus system.

After losing my car, I lost my job because I wasn't able to get to work. My money situation got really tight. I was in a severely depressive state. I had no one who would take the time to help me during these moments in my life. I had kids to feed and was not making enough to pay the bills, so I got the idea to become an exotic dancer (aka stripper). In my right state of mind, I would have never thought such a thing, but I was getting desperate!

I was so ashamed of this time in my life, I have never revealed this to anyone else until now. The only person who knew was a close friend I had at the time, and I don't recall her trying to talk me out of it. As a matter of fact, her response was, "Girl, get your money!"

I was so nervous on that first night of dancing. I don't know what I was thinking. I hadn't even graduated to having sex with the lights on, yet there I was! How was I going to be able to strip in front of strangers? I felt I needed the money, though—by *ANY* means necessary. Each night, I consumed alcohol until I could barely stand, just to block out the pain of what I was doing. Not even a week later, I decided I couldn't do it anymore. My dignity wasn't worth the tips I made. I quit and instead of looking at it as a good thing, I beat myself up about my decision. The devil made me think I was a quitter. I was so ugly, I couldn't even strip! I believed that nonsense and fell into a deeper depression. I was completely unhappy with life and myself all together.

One of the most important things we should do is hold on to our joy. We can afford to lose houses, cars, and all other material things, but we cannot afford to lose our joy. It is our joy within that will allow us to make it through the hard times, and joy can only be received by trusting God and letting Him do His will in our lives. We must hold onto our joy throughout our trials because our very lives depend on it.

"The thief comes only to steal and kill and destroy; I have come that they may have life and have it to the fullest."
(John 10:10)

"Though the fig tree does not bud and there are no grapes on the vines, though the olive crop fails, and the fields produce no food, though there are no sheep in the pen and no cattle in the stalls, yet I will rejoice in the Lord. I will be joyful in God my Savior."
(Habakkuk 3:17-18).

Even in the midst of our mistakes and struggles, God can turn them around for our good. Truthfully, when something doesn't work out, God already knew it wouldn't beforehand. HE makes the final decision, and if something is for you, it is for *YOU*.

If it were meant for Jaelon and me to be together, we would have been, despite all my efforts to push him away. He would have fought for me and helped me through what I was going through. He didn't, so he was, instead, an intricate piece of a puzzle that would teach me a lesson on life. He wasn't meant to be my husband or in my life for a lifetime. He was only meant to be present for a season. In this lifetime, there is truly a season for **E.V.E.R.Y.T.H.I.N.G.**

> "There is a time for everything, and a season for every activity under Heaven: a time to be born and a time to die, a time to plant and a time to uproot, a time to kill and a time to heal, a time to tear down and a time to build, a time to weep and a time to laugh, a time to mourn and a time to dance, a time to scatter stones and a time to gather them, a time to embrace and a time to refrain, a time to search and a time to give up, a time to keep and a time to throw away, a time to tear and a time to mend, a time to be silent and a time to speak, a time to love and a time to hate, a time for war and a time for peace."
> (Ecclesiastes 3:1-8)

God took into account every 'season' that could or would happen in our lives. He knows what we are going to do before we do it, and He already has a solution. Many times, we don't recognize it until much later, but we must learn from our experiences and try not to make the same mistakes again. The wonderful thing about God is that **HE DOESN'T MAKE MISTAKES!** Things that happen in our lives are allowed to happen so that He can change and prepare us for what is to come. If something doesn't happen the way we plan, it is because it is not in *GOD'S* plan—and He has a perfect plan for our lives!

> "For You created my inmost being; You knit me together in my mother's womb. I praise You because I am fearfully and wonderfully made; Your works are wonderful, I know that full well."
> (Psalms 139:13-14).

Put It into Practice

Even as adults, there are still some things we are insecure about. List the things you always think about or want to change. Then, refer back to the scripture that says you are fearfully and wonderfully made. Ask God to teach you how to love yourself.

_____

_____

_____

_____

_____

_____

_____

_____

_____

_____

_____

_____

_____

_____

_____

_____

_____

Lashundra Smith

How have insecurities stopped you from fulfilling your dreams or God-given purpose?

Clarity: Beauty in Pain

Think about situations in your life and ask yourself, "Did I rely on God or my own emotions?" How can you overcome this habit?

_____
_____
_____
_____
_____
_____
_____
_____
_____
_____
_____
_____
_____
_____
_____
_____
_____
_____
_____
_____
_____
_____

Lashundra Smith

As a Christian, do you believe you are not supposed to suffer? Why or why not? Review scriptures in the Bible that discuss suffering.

_____
_____
_____
_____
_____
_____
_____
_____
_____
_____
_____
_____
_____
_____
_____
_____
_____
_____
_____
_____

Judge Me Not

After getting over the heartbreak of losing Jaelon, my life began again about a year later. I was going out with my sisters and having a good time. Jaleesa met a young man named Terrell at a party we attended. Their relationship blossomed, and they grew very close. I was happy for my sister at first because of what she experienced with a previous boyfriend. He had stolen something very precious to her: her virginity. He forced himself on her, believing he had the right to do so because he was her boyfriend. After what she had endured, she deserved happiness.

Unfortunately, I started noticing traits in Terrell that I had seen too many times before in bad relationships I had. I didn't have the right to say anything to her because I allowed myself to go through those same patterns with me; however, I wanted my sister to have better, even if it wasn't my decision.

I witnessed a controlling nature in Terrell that I had seen before in others. I didn't like that he came over late to my home to see my sister, so I said something to her about it. The conversation did not go the way I envisioned and took a turn for the worst. The next morning, Terrell came bursting into my bedroom and told me I couldn't tell him when to come to see Jaleesa. I was in shock because first of all, we were in **MY** house! I thought Jaleesa would defend me and tell him he disrespected me in **MY** house. Instead, she chose to leave with him. A heated argument ensued as they were leaving out the door. I was sure she was going to stay at home with me, so when she and Teisha left, it broke my heart.

They went to my granny's house, and Jaleesa told my mother her version of the story. This included the fact that I bought one of Terrell's friends a pair of tennis shoes. I wasn't quite sure why she felt it necessary to share that, but it did open my eyes to my own level of stupidity with that choice.

Clarity: Beauty in Pain

As time progressed, Jaleesa and I regained some form of friendship. We began to work together at a bank along with another young lady named Jennifer. The two of them grew close, but I always saw Jennifer as being a troublemaker. I was comfortable enough to share with Jaleesa how I felt about Jennifer. Wouldn't you know it? My sister went back and told Jennifer all that I said!

One day while talking on the phone with my mother, I heard a knock at my door. Jennifer was on the other side. When I opened the door, she swung at me, and we started fighting on the stairs to my apartment. As we were fighting, I looked out and saw Jaleesa and Terrell sitting in the car watching us. I can't even begin to explain the level of hurt. I couldn't believe they brought her to **MY HOUSE**!

It was later explained to me that Jennifer lied and told them she just wanted to talk to me. However, I still wonder: Couldn't they have just given her my phone number? Or when they saw what she came to do, why didn't either of them get out of the car to stop her? At the time, my sister was pregnant, so I understand why *SHE* didn't jump out and intervene. But why did they bring her to **MY** home in the first place? It was an uncomfortable feeling being caught completely off guard in **MY** own home. I felt so disrespected.

It truly hurt my heart that Jaleesa never apologized for the role she played in the incident. One thing I do know well is that sometimes when we deal with the men whom we love, we allow things to happen that we usually wouldn't. It took me some time, but I forgave her.

"For if you forgive men when they sin against you, your Heavenly Father will also forgive you. But if you do not forgive men their sins, your Father will not forgive your sins."
(Matthew 6:14-15).

I also forgave myself because regardless, it was not my place to make decisions about who Jaleesa was to be with. As a sister, my only job was to be supportive. (This was something I would later find out I would need as well.) The moment we judge another, we find ourselves thinking that what they are going through is something we won't. That is the exact moment we have set ourselves up for failure.

"Do not judge or you, too, will be judged. For in the same way you judge others, you will be judged, and with the measure you use, it will be measured to you. Why do you look at the speck of sawdust in your brother's eye and pay no attention t the plank in your own eye? How can you say to your brother, 'Let me take the speck out of your eye,' when all the time there is a plank in your own eye? You hypocrite, first take the plank out of your own eye, and then you will see clearly to remove the speck from your brother's eye."
(Matthew 7:1-5)

Nobody is above finding themselves in a toxic relationship. Most often, it's not an intentional choice. We want to believe the person we fall in love with is right for us.

So, while I was judging who my sister was seeing, I was being foolish myself. I was dating guys who didn't give one care about me and, in the process, was trying to buy their affections. Meanwhile, my family and friends were talking about me and calling me "stupid" instead of pulling me to the side and having a serious tough-love talk with me.

I felt isolated again. Everyone around me had a boyfriend or was in a stable relationship. I found myself admiring even the bad relationships, even the ones I knew had cheating mates. "At least they have a man," were among my list of odd thoughts. I felt and acted as I had no one when I actually had two beautiful children to care for. Instead of focusing on my kids and their needs and showing my daughter the affection she required, I showed them an unhappy mother with no self-worth and low self-esteem. Although my daughter was very young and likely doesn't remember any of what I went through, I believe those spirits can escape and enter our children. The Bible speaks of evil spirits jumping into and onto others on several occasions. One account is dealing with the Jews in the Book of Acts:

> **"Some Jews who went around driving out evil spirits tried to invoke the name of the Lord Jesus over those who were demon-possessed. They would say, 'In the name of Jesus whom Paul preaches, I command you to come out!' Seven sons of Sceva, a Jewish chief priest, were doing this. One day, the evil spirit answered them. 'Jesus I know, and Paul I know about, but who are you?' The man who had the evil spirit jumped on them and overpowered them all. He gave them such a beating that they ran out of the house naked and bleeding."**
> (Acts 9:13-16)

I was so unhappy, I didn't know how to love my kids. I didn't even know how to love myself. I sunk deeper and deeper into depression, lowering my expectations in men each time. I convinced myself that if I lowered my standards enough, I could get it right for once. All the feelings I had for men I dated were superficial. I focused on looks instead of character traits. If they didn't look a certain way, I didn't give them the time of day. I pushed the nice ones away in exchange for the ones everyone else wanted. I was in love with the idea of being in love.

> **"The goal of this command is love, which comes from a pure heart and a good conscience and sincere faith."**
> (1 Timothy 1:5)

Half the time, the men I chose to be with were only because they chose to be with me. I consistently lowered my standards of how I should have been treated. Anything that looked presentable to me, I accepted. I sunk to a new level by dating Dewayne, a boy right out of high school. He was at least for years younger than me. I let the excitement he showed me by dating an older woman cloud my judgment. I convinced myself we were headed in the right direction. We spent a lot of time together both in person and talking on the phone. I was falling in love with a BOY! Clearly, he was not mature enough to be a man.

Before I knew it, I was pregnant again!

The moment he found out, his true colors appeared. His immaturity. Check! His insensitivity. Double check. His downright ignorance. Triple check! He started ignoring me and wouldn't return my phone calls. Note here that I was already having problems with this pregnancy, likely due to all the stress. I ended up going to the hospital because of pains and bleeding. I was informed the baby was developing in my fallopian tube and was immediately rushed into surgery. Imagine my surprise when I woke up after the procedure, and they told me I was still pregnant! Apparently, the diagnosis was an error; it was **NOT** a tubal pregnancy! They had to be sure, though, so they had to open me up so that I would not bleed internally.

This life cycle of mine seemed to be a never-ending battle!

I decided then and there that I couldn't have the baby. The enemy had me convinced this was a sign to get rid of it. I called Dewayne, giving him the opportunity to stop me from following through. I thought my call would wake him up and come running to my side. Well, he didn't care. He wouldn't even go to the abortion clinic with me. Jaleesa ended up going with me for support. I felt I made the best decision for me at the time. I already had two kids and no one to help me raise them. The baby would be better off not entering this world (at least that's what I told myself). However, that one decision made me a murderer. The enemy had won again! I punished myself for years behind the decision I made, furthering the success of the enemy's mission to keep me in a despondent state of mind.

Life dragged on. I went from job to job due to a lack of reliable transportation, a reliance on the bus system, and unreliable babysitting arrangements. For months, I awoke at dawn, walked a mile through a very bad neighborhood named Oakcliff to drop the kids off at the nearest daycare, and then made the return trip home to catch the bus to get to work. Most days, I didn't know whether I was coming or going. I smiled and pretended all was okay. I was mentally lost and in a daze with no direction.

Not thinking rationally, I relocated to an unsafe environment. My house sat in the backwoods of a ridiculously long driveway. I didn't have a phone, so the only way I communicated with others was when they came over to my home. After realizing the position I placed my children and me in, I asked the landlord to be let out of the lease. He, of course, said no! I had no way of getting out of this mess. I didn't have a real relationship with God, but I did fear Him and began to pray to Him. Once again, God was coming to save me!

"As a father has compassion on his children, so the Lord has compassion on those who fear Him; for He knows how we are formed, He remembers that we are dust."
(Psalms 103:13-14)

After about six months of residing in the house, I awoke one morning to find my oldest child waddling in water up to his neck. I swung my legs over and realized the house was knee-deep in water. It has been raining for days, and there was a now overflowing creek right next to my home. The water destroyed all of my furniture and clothes. Everything was unsalvageable. I recall being so calm at that time for no apparent reason. I grabbed my children under both arms and ran to a nearby church to call my dad to come and pick us up.

After safely getting out of the house, my rush of adrenaline slowed and I broke down in tears. I remember screaming aloud, **"GOD, ARE YOU FOR REAL? WHY ARE YOU TORTURING ME?"** It wasn't until much later I would realize the flood was all in God's plans.

Sometimes, you have to lose everything and reach rock-bottom in order to propel to the top again.

I hated living in that neighborhood, but I was bound by a lease and could not break it. If I broke the lease, I would have lost my housing assistance—something I desperately needed at the time. The flood did not come to take our lives but to deliver me out of the disaster I was in. Yes, it took all the material things we had, but it saved my children and me from future pain. I can't help but think that the flood also saved our very lives from an unknown danger. God was still watching over me, though I didn't deserve it. He didn't allow my son to drown while I was sleeping. He saved our lives by waking me up! He removed me from a neighborhood where women were getting raped and killed. He kept me safe when I walked my kids in the dark through that bad neighborhood to daycare and back when I walked alone to the bus stop. He saved my ungrateful, unworthy, undeserving life. At the time, I still did not get it. Instead of focusing on those good things, I focused on all I had lost.

I was on a rollercoaster of emotions, deciding I was destined to live a miserable life. Why even bother to try and do better? I had to move back in with my father—the very man I had yet to forgive—and a mother I was still upset with. I was angry, ungrateful, and anxious to move back out. I was so eager that when the opportunity presented itself six months later, I moved without an ounce of furniture. My children and I slept and ate on the floor for almost a year until most of the furniture we did have was given to us. I once again made a decision based on my emotions; not one of rational thinking.

Everything that happened so far was God trying to get my attention. I missed the clues, the hints, and Him basically slapping me upside my head! He was trying to make me see what was important: HIM. He was determined to get my soul, even if that meant taking everything but my life from me. All God wanted was for me to turn to Him so He could give me peace.

"Come to Me, all you who are weary and burdened, and I will give you rest. Take My yoke upon you and learn from Me, for I am gentle and humble in heart and you will find rest for your souls. For My yoke is easy and My burden is light."
(Matthew 11:28-30)

Years of unsuccessful romantic relationships led me to bad friendships as well. I assumed I was too focused on the wrong thing; men. I needed to rearrange the attention I was giving my friends. Once again, I was not focusing my attention on God. I kept turning my trust to man. They consistently let me down, leaving me to be the one suffering...alone.

"This is what the Lord says: 'Cursed is the one who trusts in man, who depends on flesh for his strength and whose heart turns away from the Lord'."
(Jeremiah 17:5)

Being naïve, I began to put all my efforts into the friends I had. I was always available to them, had money to lend, and was a shoulder they could lean on. I would go places and be around people I didn't care for and they, in turn, didn't care a thing about me. I just wanted to be in someone's presence. I was searching for a feeling that no man or woman on earth could give me.

I would host gatherings so that people would come around and be disappointed when no one showed up. They were all one-sided friendships. I showed up and was always accessible; they weren't. To build others up, I was made to feel less than them. I actually admired them, not knowing that they were, in fact, jealous of me. As long as I was miserable, they were content with that. The moment I would stand out, speak my mind, and love myself, the so-called friendships would soon fall apart at the seams.

During this time in my life, I was blissfully unaware of all that was going on around me. I kept reaching out, wanting to be accepted by anyone who would accept me, even if that meant hanging back in the shadows. I would ignore the stares and uneasiness others experienced when I came around and assumed if I just kept giving and giving, it would one day be given back. Instead, my giving nature was draining me and constantly reminding me of my low self-esteem. It was keeping me right where the enemy wanted me: at the bottom. I would celebrate their special occasions as if they were my own. However, when my special days came around (such as my birthday), I would be lucky to have a couple of people show up. I didn't know that friendships were comprised of two people who walk beside each other, not one behind another.

"As iron sharpens iron, so one man sharpens another."
(Proverbs 27:17)

I tried to put myself in the mentality of "friends" surrounding me. I decided to be a player: do men wrong before they did me wrong. I tried to convince myself that I could block out what I truly desired. I began to envy my best friend, Nikki, and how she could just take what she wanted from men and move on. I wanted to be like her and simply not care about anyone or anything. Envy, however, is never a good thing because it causes you to be something you are not.

> **"And I saw that all labor and all achievement spring from man's envy of his neighbor. This, too, is meaningless; a chasing after the wind."**
> (Ecclesiastes 4:4)

The life Nikki and I started to live involved going to the club all the time. We spent more time trying to find babysitters for our kids than actually raising them. At the time, I am sure we thought we were good parents. We left our kids with people we trusted, but that was irrelevant. Our children needed to be raised and loved by us, not other people. Yes, we went to work daily. Yes, we provided for them and met their needs. But they were not our priority. We were both young, still marching into adulthood, and allowing the "streets" to raise us. There was a lot of competition between us as well. Neither of us would admit it at the time, but there were qualities each of us possessed that the other desired. This affected our friendship significantly—in a negative way.

I can't remember when or how it started, but the competitiveness got extremely out of hand. Where I believed boyfriends were off limits, it seemed there were no boundaries concerning any man according to Nikki. Clearly, we didn't appreciate each other as we should have. As I reflect now, I know I played a big part because when Nikki hurt me, I kept it bottled up inside. When certain comments were made, or her friends made me feel uncomfortable, I just held it in. I would talk to my other friends about it and express my hurt to them when I should have been speaking to my best friend. I believe I always wanted to avoid confrontation, leaving me to feel like even if I did say something to Nikki, she wouldn't understand, deny it, or be upset with me. I didn't want to lose her friendship, so I thought I was doing the right thing by being quiet.

Hurt is hurt, no matter how or if the other person feels they hurt you or not.

I should have talked to my best friend and given her the opportunity to fix the situation before letting things get out of hand. Instead, we let this behavior go on for years. We went back and forth with our friendship; one moment being friends, the next not. Many times, we stopped speaking to each other without even telling the other person why. I spent years in a friendship feeling like I wasn't good enough. I spent so much time trying to be like somebody else instead of being who God designed me to be. After years of this behavior, the relationship was destroyed. Eventually, we just went our separate ways. Fifteen years of friendship had been flushed down the drain, diminished to the point of cordial greetings and nothing more.

I must admit: I had hopes that we would be friends forever, but friends sometimes grow apart. They may have different goals and desires and beliefs change. The choice to choose God over sinful behaviors also breaks friends apart because they become unequally yoked.

> "Do not be yoked together with unbelievers. For what do righteousness and wickedness have in common? Or what fellowship can light have with darkness? What harmony is there between Christ and Belial? Or what does a believer have in common with an unbeliever? What agreement is there between the temple of God and idols? For we are the temple of the Living God. As God has said, 'I will live with them and walk among them, and I will be their God, and they will be My people.' Therefore, 'Come out from them and be separate,' says the Lord."
> (2 Corinthians 6:14-17)

When God has plans for you, and you are different, He will not allow those around you to stay if they hinder your growth in Him. There will always be feuding and confusion amongst you because you are not operating in divine connections.

Not only did Nikki and I grow apart, but we were becoming different people. I feel we did need to go our separate ways so that both of us could develop in the direction in which God would have for us. Also, we needed to work on forgiving one another. We blamed each other for many things and never truly forgave one another. Each time one did something to hurt the other, we held onto it. We would begin talking again right where we left off, with neither one forgiving the other before moving forward. I remember thinking, "How many times can you forgive someone for the same thing?!" Again, God's Word has **ALL** the answers to our questions:

> "Then, Peter came to Jesus and asked, 'Lord, how many times shall I forgive my brother or sister who sins against me? Up to seven times?' Jesus answered, 'I tell you, not seven times, but seventy-seven times'."
> (Matthew 18:21-22)

It became evident to me that I needed to work on forgiveness to maintain relationships. People are bound to hurt you—likely more than once—and to keep a relationship in good standing, you have to practice genuine forgiveness at some point. Now, this does **NOT** mean you have to be a footstool, but you have to either forgive and move on **OR** forgive and hold on (if you feel it's worth it).

I desired a healthy friendship with Nikki; one in which we could grow together. We vowed that when we were both financially stable, we would take trips, go shopping, and have weekly lunch dates together. We were supposed to be in each other's wedding, but that wasn't going to happen.

Friends are supposed to love each other through our flaws. However, when we neglect to communicate, we open up doors for the enemy to creep in and destroy us. He can quickly get the upper hand by causing division and confusion in the relationship. Every relationship requires communication—not just marriages, but friendships as well. Many times, someone is bound to do something to the other that will cause strife. After all, we are only human. The Bible gives us guidance as to how relationships should work, if only we would follow God's Word.

"Therefore, as God's chosen people, holy and dearly loved, clothe yourselves with compassion, kindness, humility, gentleness, and patience. Bear with each other and forgive whatever grievances you may have against one another. Forgive as the Lord forgave you. And over all these virtues, put on love, which binds them all together in perfect unity."
(Colossians 3:12-14)

The friendship Nikki and I shared was both priceless and taken for granted. We eventually connected again and are now cherishing the relationship we have. God can mend anything He wants to be mended. He separated us for a time to allow us to grow individually and learn how to be true friends to one another.

As life went on, I found out that God-given friendships are divine connections. A friend is one who prays for you, is there for you, and is genuinely happy for you. You can trust them to be there when it really counts and let you shine when it's your turn to shine.

"Be good friends who love deeply; practice playing second fiddle."
(Romans 12:10)

A friend will make mistakes, but real friends can forgive each other and agree to disagree. Friends celebrate each other's achievements and are genuinely sad when the other is going through a hard time. God is the **BEST** friend you could ever have and, if you are fortunate, He will send good earthly friends to walk your journey with you.

"Truly, truly, I say to you, whoever hears My Word and believes Him who sent Me has eternal life. He does not come into judgment but has passed from death to life."
(Matthew 12:36-37)

Put It into Practice

Carefully consider the following question and note your honest answer below: Are you judgmental in any way whatsoever? If you are unsure, ask God to reveal it to you.

_____
_____
_____
_____
_____
_____
_____
_____
_____
_____
_____
_____
_____
_____
_____
_____

Clarity: Beauty in Pain

Once you identify ways in which you are judgmental, in what ways can you overcome this? One option is to look at yourself and identify areas you feel needs improvement. Then, ask yourself, "Would I want others to judge me in those areas?"

_____

_____

_____

_____

_____

_____

_____

_____

_____

_____

_____

_____

_____

_____

_____

_____

_____

_____

_____

_____

Have you ever made a decision you regret? After you identify those decisions, how does this help you not to judge others for their choices?

There is Only One God

While out clubbing with Nikki, I met my youngest son's father, William. He was charming and handsome. He said all the things I wanted to hear. He had game I wasn't up on yet, and found myself falling for each line he fed me. I immediately fell for him and what was meant to be just a fling turned out to us living together. Before I knew it, he was dropping me off at work and driving my car.

The first few weeks we were together, I got a hold of his phone and discovered he already had a girlfriend. I was confused, considering he was always at my house. How could he have a girlfriend? I assumed she was lying at first, until she told me what kind of car I had. As I held the phone in disbelief, she explained to me how he had been driving my car to her house to see her while I was at work. She said he told her it was his car, but when I answered his phone, she immediately knew he was lying.

When he got home, I confronted him about it, and he told me, "I admit we were together, but I met you and fell for you. I am ending the relationship right now because I don't want to lose you. Feeling like this is new to me. I was confused at first, but I now know that it's over between her and me."

Well, you guessed right if you thought, "Shunda fell for it!"

I had my chance to leave the relationship right then, but like an idiot, I believed him and ignored every red flag thrown at me. I purposely pressed the **"IGNORE"** button. I ignored the times he didn't answer his phone and the nights he wouldn't come home to me. I desperately wanted to love him and for him to love me. I was tired of the rollercoaster ride of men in and out of my life. My heart yelled, *"ENOUGH ALREADY!"* William stuck around, and I accepted it as love. He didn't work but was always "looking for work." At the time, I was caring for him, feeding him, and putting gas in my car for **HIM** to drive around…"looking for work."

In a moment of blatant transparency here, I didn't understand (at first) why he chose to remain in the relationship. I came to realize that his sticking around wasn't love; it was him using me. He took and took and took, and gave nothing in return.

Weeks turned into months. I remained in this unhealthy relationship and gave excuses for why he was still with me. At least he could babysit the kids when the need arose. In front of me, he acted as though he loved them. Before I knew it, I was putting him before everything.

"You shall not make for yourself an idol in the form of anything in Heaven above or on the earth beneath or in the waters below. You shall not bow down to them or worship them; for I, the Lord your God, am a jealous God, punishing the children for the sins of the fathers to the third and fourth generation of those who hate Me."
(Exodus 20:3-5)

Unknowingly, I was worshipping a man. I made him my priority, doing whatever it took to please him. I wanted to be whatever he wanted me to be. He would often verbally abuse me by reminding me how skinny I was. In response, I desperately tried to gain weight. I was doing anything I could to make him want and desire me, even trying to be better in bed sexually.

I ended up getting pregnant again, so now I had three children with three different fathers—and William would not let me forget it. He knew I didn't want to separate from another one of my children's fathers. I had mentioned to him many times before that if I got pregnant again, I was staying with whoever I was with and that I would **NOT** go through it alone again, no matter what it took. The verbal onslaughts continued because he knew my weakness. When we would argue, he used the opportunity to remind me that no other man would want me with other men's children in tow. He also told me I was useless, ugly, and full of baggage.

I let him come and go as he pleased. He refused to work, leaving me to pay all the bills. What he did do was sit at home and talk to other women all day long, unbeknownst to me. Deep in my heart, I felt he was cheating but chose to ignore my feelings. I attributed my suspicions based on paranoia from past wrongs and relationships gone bad. I kept telling myself I had no proof anyway. I should have followed my intuition. I remained hopeful that he would get a job soon and believed him when he said that while he was out, he was completing applications.

It wasn't long before he gave me a sexually-transmitted disease. He, of course, blamed me for it saying I had to have had it before or was cheating on him. I knew I hadn't cheated on him, so that wasn't it. So, I went for the lame excuse, even though I hadn't been with anyone since my last boyfriend. I told myself the symptoms were just late since I showed no signs of being infected before that moment. I also ignored the check-up I had before we met that came back negative of all diseases.

I was seriously in a state of outright denial.

The neighbors watched, whispered, and laughed at me. His own mother even played along, acting as if she was crazy about me, too, to get what she wanted as well.

As I said, I was pregnant again and chose to keep the baby. I refused to have another abortion. I loved William and was sticking this thing out for better or worse. I was following the rules of a marriage to a man who was not even my husband. I would go to work and allow him to keep the car all day, thinking he was looking for a job. I would often wait for him for hours after I got off work looking foolish. Repeatedly, I turned down offers for rides home, telling people I had a ride while making up lies for why he was late picking me up. We would argue all the way home, with him always finding a way to turn it all on me…and I would fall for it every time. Somehow, I would end up being the one to apologize to him after the argument, and he was the one who was late!

During my pregnancy, he would leave for days at a time. A neighbor named Cynthia would constantly pick and nag at me whenever I came outside. I couldn't understand why. She was still in high school and lived two doors down from me. I was naïve enough to think that there was **NO** way he could be **THAT** bold to sleep with a child. I had no idea he was, indeed, having sex with her. The neighbors finally got sick and tired of it and told me what was going on.

I sat in disbelief listening as another neighbor told me that when I would leave for work, Cynthia was in my home. When William would say to me he was going to spend time with his friend Chris, he would drive up to the stop sign at the corner and Cynthia would hop into the truck with them.

I couldn't believe what I heard! Surely, they were lying!

When confronted about it, William stressed to me, "None of it is true, baby. Cynthia is jealous. I used to talk to her before you, and I got together. When we moved on this street, I wanted to tell you but didn't want you to be worried about her. We were long broken up prior to moving here. Don't let them ruin what we have with their lies."

I had to…I wanted to believe him. I was already four months pregnant at the time.

The stories about one woman after the next wouldn't stop coming, though. One even called and told me she had sex with William while my daughter sat in the living room waiting on them to finish. These women had no respect for themselves or me. The cycle seemed to be constant, and I just kept burying the other women away like they didn't exist.

One particular incident that comes to mind was when he brought a "childhood friend" named Natalie into our home. He claimed they were just hanging out and catching up on old times. He even carried her picture in his wallet. I knew what was up, though. I could tell by the way he was holding the picture and gazing at it that there was more to the story.

When I was six months pregnant, I was still dealing with the foolishness. As was customary by this time, he picked a fight so that he could leave the house. He would stay out all night with the excuse that he was upset and didn't want to come home. I knew he had been with Natalie, but I said nothing. After all, he was back home. That was what was most important to me.

Then, all that I feared the most came to light.

The next morning, I heard screaming and someone erratically honking the horn outside my front door. "William, come out! William, come out now!" yelled some girl standing outside my house.

I peeked out the blind, trying to see what the commotion was all about. I turned to look at William with an expression that said, "Fool! I **KNOW** you don't have someone outside my house acting like a nutcase!"

Clarity: Beauty in Pain

William got up, looked out the window, and shrugged. We both walked to the door. I remember the frantic woman from the picture he showed me. It was his "childhood friend," Natalie. She was standing next to a car with his best friend, Chris, sitting inside. I couldn't believe he brought her to my home! Chris was apologetic and said, "She made me bring her here."

I asked her what she wanted, prepared to fight due to the total disrespect of showing up at my home. She must have somehow known my intent because she stood behind the car talking crazy and telling me that William told her he was leaving me. She wanted to know why he was back at the house with me.

William glanced over at me and began to walk towards her. He had the audacity to get in the car with her! I was in shock! I just knew my eyes **MUST** have been deceiving me. They drove off with Chris behind the wheel.

I ran down the street chasing after the car, begging him to stay. As I watched the car drive away, I screamed as tears stroked my cheeks, "Please, don't leave me like this with your son!" William never looked back.

Once I realized he was gone with her and not coming back, I think time froze for several seconds. I couldn't move or barely breathe. He did it. He had left me alone and six months pregnant with his child. All the commotion had drawn out the curious neighbors, all who witnessed a woman show up and leave with my man.

Talk about pain, hurt, frustration, and anger! I don't think I have ever been as angry again as I was on that day. In my rage, I found a brick and threw it through the front window of his car. I then grabbed a butcher knife and played tic-tac-toe on the sides of his car. Yes, I was out of my mind. I lost it! I can't believe I allowed a man to take me to that level.

When someone can make you that angry, you have truly given them way too much power over you.

To this day, I thank God that William had left because I honestly believe I would have killed him.

After the anger subsided and it sunk in what just happened, the tears slowly rolled down my face. I looked at what I did to the car and knew I was out of my mind. At that moment, I realized that once again, I would be raising another man's child alone. He left me when I needed him the most: when I was pregnant with his only son. I cried myself to sleep every single night until my child was born.

How easy would it have been to turn my worries to God and let Him lift the heavy burdens I felt?

"Humble yourselves, therefore, under God's mighty hand, that He may lift you up in due time. Cast all your anxiety on Him because He cares for you."
(1 Peter 5:6-7)

God cared for me while I was chasing a man around who couldn't care less. If only I knew then what I know now…

At my son Kyjuan's birth, William showed up. He didn't even have the decency to come alone. He brought Natalie. Fortunately for both of them, I didn't see her. A friend told me that she was there. Still, it didn't make knowing she was around any better than not seeing her in the flesh. William continued to show no respect for me, and I continued to ignore it. He ended up spending the night with me in the hospital and filled my head with lies. He said he made a mistake and wanted to work out our relationship for our family. I wanted to believe that was true, so I decided to forgive him. I couldn't raise another child without the father being present. I fell for his lies and let him move back in. Deep in my heart, I knew the peace between us would only last a moment.

Not long after our reunion, the emotional and verbal abuse turned physical, as if him reminding me that nobody else wanted me wasn't enough. At first, he would grab my arm tightly and shove me. The yelling and threats then began to be accompanied by a slap across my face. At times, he would push my tiny frame so hard, I would fall to the ground. I made the abuse worse when I would talk back or try to defend myself. Those times, he would put his hands around my neck and choke me so hard, I would lose consciousness for seconds at a time. At one point, I recall him being so angry, he wrapped a telephone cord around my neck, causing me to take life-saving grasps at the cord to release the pressure and get air into my lungs.

I would put him out each time, and he would call crying and begging to come back home, promising it was the last time. I remember one summer day deciding I was done with the arguments. As he was yelling and screaming obscenities at me, I turned to walk away while telling him to leave.

Several minutes later, I awoke on the couch in our living room confused. I tried to lift my head, but it felt like it weighed a ton. I began to slowly turn my head to look around me and noticed a huge hole caved into the wall that looked like a silhouette of my body.

I kept asking him over and over again, "What happened? What did you do?"

He seemed nervous as he kept pacing back and forth, yelling at me to stop asking questions and to quit playing like something was wrong with me. I tried to tell him I really needed help, but he grabbed my car keys and left me there with my two older kids and his seven-month-old son who was crawling around on the floor.

Once my thoughts began to clear, I realized he had pushed me into the wall. His nervousness was because I am sure he assumed I was dead when I wasn't responding. All at once, I blacked out again. I kept going in and out of consciousness. Although I didn't want to, I had to call my mother. I couldn't be alone with the kids while suffering the after-effects of the abuse. My parents came right over and drove me to the hospital. My father was prepared to kill William.

To God be the glory, his family would not tell my father where he was.

When I arrived at the hospital, I was diagnosed with a slight concussion and told I would be fine. The police were called, but I refused to tell them anything. Even after the severity of the abuse, I just couldn't send him to jail. He was, after all, my son's father.

I made a promise to my parents that I wouldn't allow William back in my home, and I truly believed it when I made that promise. I honestly thought my mind was finally made up, and it was…for about two months. Around that two-month mark, he said all the right things. He told me he didn't realize he would ever go that far and that he would control his anger, get help, and do whatever he needed to do to make us work. He seemed so sincere. I let him back into our home, with the relationship maintaining its sense of normalcy. He was polite and stayed at home, versus being obnoxious and staying away from home for days at a time. He even got a job!

I was sure I had made the right choice. I told myself we got off to a rough start but that people can change.

Well, even after all of his changes, I couldn't stand for him to touch me. I was like a robot when we had sex. There was no emotion behind the act. So much damage had been done to my psyche, I didn't know how to allow myself to feel again. I felt empty, like a big hole took residence in my heart.

I realized that God was the missing piece in my life. I began to attend church and grew a personal relationship with God. I didn't quite believe in Him fully, but I was definitely interested. I started to pray and ask for guidance. I specifically asked God to show me that William was not for me, without a shadow of a doubt (as if He hadn't shown me already). I was honest with God and told Him I couldn't see it for myself. I needed for Him to allow William to do something to cause me to feel so foolish, I couldn't take him back even if I wanted to.

Be very careful what you pray for!

Since William had gotten a job, I felt he needed a car. I took my son's disability check that was typically used to pay our utility bills and bought him a car. He promised he would give the money back the very next time he got paid. I reiterated that we needed the money for bills and to not let his family down. He agreed. Friday morning of that week, we went to pick out a car. He chose a white Ford Tempo. I remember being so excited, thinking we were finally headed in the right direction!

That same night at around 10:00 p.m., we were watching television when William looked at me and said, "Man, I want some ice cream. What about you?"

"Yes," I said. "That would be good! Go get us some!"

He left to go on the ice cream run and time ticked by.

11:00 p.m.

Midnight.

1:00 a.m.

At 2:00 a.m., I became frantic. I called the jails and hospitals, thinking something horrible happened. I couldn't sleep, and his mother wasn't answering the phone. We were doing so well, I just knew something awful had to have happened to him.

At 9:00 a.m., he came waltzing through the door with no explanation. He acted as if going out for ice cream and coming back ten hours later was perfectly fine. When I asked him where he had been, he had the **NERVE** to be upset! He grabbed his clothes and all his personal items while I yelled behind him the entire time. He walked outside with his stuff in hand, and I followed closely behind, continuing to yell and scream. I had our baby in my arm, and he pushed both of us down to the concrete driveway. He climbed into the car and drove away, only to call me minutes later saying the car had stalled.

God truly doesn't like ugly!

I didn't respond. At that point, I didn't care. The problem ended up being that the transmission went out in the car. The car lot allowed him to come back and get a replacement car, though.

Even after all this, there is no telling what I would have done. I believe in my heart, however, that God knew I would take him back again if something serious didn't happen quickly. God chose that moment to begin working in my life in regards to the prayer I prayed about William. God is a jealous God and would no longer allow me to worship a man!

> **"You shall not bow down to them or worship them;
> for I, the LORD our God, am a jealous God, punishing the children
> for the sins of the fathers to the third and
> fourth generation of those who hate Me."**
> (Exodus 20:5)

Days later, my water was cut off. William wouldn't give me the money back that I gave him for the car, even after I told him my situation. His words were, "It's not my responsibility!" He obviously didn't care that his son's formula required **WATER**. He didn't care that we needed **WATER** to bathe and drink. He sat on the other end of the phone line with nothing but sarcasm in his voice. He seemed to have so much disgust for us. I could hear it in his voice. He was irritated and uncaring. It was as if our relationship never existed. Even *THEN*, I believe I would have taken him back, so God began to put into action the answer to my prayer.

A few weeks later, William volunteered up his car for me to use to take Kyjuan to his doctor's appointment. After the appointment, I just so happened to look in the trunk and found a woman's hair weave. With confusion, I began digging through the trunk further and found a pair of women's heels and Medicaid papers. I looked at the name and recognized it as an old classmate, Sheniqua. Not only was she a former classmate, but she was also on the list of females one of my ex-boyfriends cheated with. I was angry beyond comprehension. I went to the address on the paperwork, and her mother answered the door. She looked past me and out toward the driveway. "Why are you driving my daughter's car?" she asked.

I shockingly replied, "There's no way this could be your daughter's car, considering I am the one who put the down payment on the car in the first place!"

Reality struck as I overheard Sheniqua's mother telling her I was driving her car. As I stood there, I couldn't understand how a man could be so cruel. How could he look me in my eyes all those years, say he loves me, and do this? I was the mother of his first child! Sheniqua was blindsided and didn't understand what was going on either. She explained to me that she didn't even know I existed. She went on to say that when the other car broke down, he took **HER** to the lot and allowed her to pick out the new car, saying it was *FOR HER*! She volunteered to go with me to his job to confront him. Well, the surprise ended up being on me!

When we arrived, he stood there with this stupid grin on his face. At first, he tried to ignore us. Sheniqua began telling him off, and I was (at first) too stunned to say anything at all. When I finally gathered my thoughts, he had the nerve to tell me I had no right to question him! We had only been broken up all of two weeks, yet I had no right to question him? Sheniqua was staying at his mother's house with him, and I had no right to question him? We argued back and forth for a moment before he reached out and slapped me! Right in front of another woman, he put his hands on me! He then reached into the car, grabbed my son's car seat, set it on the curb, spit on his son and me, and drove away with Sheniqua riding shotgun in the car.

He spat on us like we were merely another part of the concrete. It was the most humiliating moment of my life. I had to call my older sister to pick us up. I was so ashamed to have to call someone and say, "Come to get me because my son's father left me on the side of the road." I cried uncontrollably. My body was shaking all over, as if I was about to have a seizure. I had never felt such pain, uncontrollable hurt, and rage.

This was "it"! This was exactly what I prayed to God for. Although there were prayers before that I knew God answered, this was the first time I took notice. He had to bring me to my worst for me to know He was there.

I would not and could not take William back even if I wanted to. This was the point of no return. However, I forgot to ask God to help me not to hate him. I forgot to forgive him, knowing that even if I knew I should at that moment, I don't believe I would have. I had to let him go physically but he still had control over me through my hatred and unforgiveness.

He was in and out of my son's life. The same kids who used to call him 'daddy,' he no longer had anything to do with. He would lie to his new girlfriend and say he was bringing diapers over for our son, knowing he had no intentions of stopping by. His abuse was never-ending, even though he was no longer in my home. He would cuss me out when he picked up his son if I acted like I wanted nothing to do with him. He even hit me in the mouth, busting my lip in the process in front of her because I told the truth: he hadn't brought **ANY** diapers to my son — ever!

My hatred for William grew and grew. As a consequence, I trusted no men and didn't care if they had multiple women because I had no intention of getting serious with them anyway. I was disrespectful, mean, and hateful towards all men. The emptiness filtered back into my heart. I was living a lie. I told myself my actions were okay and that the walls I built up were there to protect me when the truth was that in my heart, I have always desired a meaningful relationship.

Today, I look back on the relationship with William and realize I was also partly to blame. Many things that he did, I allowed. I had the freedom to walk away at any given time. I, however, allowed past circumstances to taint my judgment. I should have done a background check on him before I allowed him into my life, my heart, my kids' lives, or my home. Note that a background check is not limited to criminal history. As a matter of fact, even if something is on someone's background, that doesn't necessarily make them a bad person. When I say 'background check,' I am referring to their family and upbringing. You can learn a lot about a man just by asking him how his childhood was. Listen closely to how he discusses his parents' relationship. Ask him how long his parents are or were married. Did they argue often? How did your father treat your mother? The responses will indicate how he will treat you.

As for William, his parents were not together. His mother gave custody to his father, so William was angry at women in general. He has no respect for them because of what his mother did.

Now, there are men out there who see how their father hurt their mother and they react the exact opposite, but that doesn't happen often. The moment you see any indications in the man you are dating that what he told you about his past begins to shine through, it shouldn't be hard to determine you are getting yourself into the same type of relationship. Selfishness, bitterness, and anger are not achieved overnight. They are attributes that slowly progress due to circumstances life has thrown at us, and we didn't know any other way to handle them. When those signs appear, it is not the time for you to believe you will be the agent of change to save that person.

So many times, it's easy to believe we can change a person. Have you ever thought, "If I just love them a little harder, they will change"? Unfortunately, the person has to want to change first and needs time to heal from whatever they have experienced. We cannot force change on them. In fact, it often pushes them to the deep end. We must learn not to become other people's 'god.' We are not God; there is only one, and He is the **ONLY** one who can get into someone's heart and provide true correction.

This relationship also taught me about friends and how people are so quick to judge others. When I was in the relationship with William, I isolated myself from others because I was embarrassed. I didn't care how I looked anymore due to allowing his very words to change my identity. I no longer desired to dress up cute or comb my hair. When I tried, he made it a point to tell me I wasn't beautiful anyway, so why try? I hated my body shape because he said I was too skinny, prompting me to desperately want to gain weight. Instead of my friends reaching out to me and shaking me back to reality, they just talked about me. I didn't need to be talked about; I needed someone to grab me and say, "Friend, you are beautiful. You don't have to take that from him." I needed someone to show me that I deserved more instead of telling their other friends how stupid I was.

We all need tough love at times. Somebody has to stand up and not be afraid of the anger that may arise because of that tough love lesson. It's likely the recipient will be upset, but the moment they come to their senses, they will respect you so much more for being that friend who stood up and said what needed to be heard. It's so easy and cowardly to point the finger at someone when they are going through rough times. It takes courage and a spirit of God to say to that person, "You are beautiful. I don't know what happened to you or why you do the things you are doing, but I love you anyway." God can use you to show people who are at their worst that God still loves them.

Lashundra Smith

"Therefore, my dear friends; flee from idolatry."
(1 Corinthians 10:14)

Put It into Practice

What are your idols? Truly self-reflect and ask yourself, "What idols am I worshipping?" List them here. God is a jealous God. Ask Him to help you understand that He is the only one you should be worshipping.

_____

_____

_____

_____

_____

_____

_____

_____

_____

_____

_____

_____

_____

_____

_____

_____

_____

_____

_____

Lashundra Smith

Describe abuse in your own words. Based on your description, have you ever been abused or are you being abused at this time?

Clarity: Beauty in Pain

Now that you have identified abuse, what are your next steps? Do you have someone you can talk to such as a minster or trustworthy friend?

If you have children, how do you believe it affects them to see you being abused?

Yes, Jesus Loves Me

Again, God began to speak to my heart. He loved me! Yes, He knew all the things I had done, yet he **STILL** loved me!

"For I am convinced that neither death nor life, neither angels nor demons, neither present nor the future, nor any powers, neither height nor depth, nor anything else in all creation, will be able to separate us from the love of God that is in Christ Jesus our Lord."
(Romans 8:38-39)

I began to seek Him, try Him out, and get to know Him. I began to hope again and believe that love really existed. I recalled how He got me through so many rough times, recognizing the moments that could have only been God. I began to appreciate my worth; the beauty and talents that existed in me. I began to dream and hope again and started to plan for the future!

"The Lord makes firm the steps of the one who delights in Him; though he may stumble, he will not fall, for the Lord upholds him with His hand."
(Psalms 37:23-24)

God began to order my steps and desires. I no longer desired other people's leftovers—those men who didn't care about my children or me. I wanted what **GOD** had for me.

During this time, I started to take myself out on dates. I would go out to eat and to the movies alone. I still went out with others but found myself able to go and have a good time without the company of others all the time. I didn't need a man to talk to me or define who I was as a woman any longer.

One of those nights, I met one of my closest friends, Tashia. She approached me as I was watching others dance and have a good time. She explained to me she had just lost her grandfather and uncle around the same time. Tashia needed a friend at that moment.

Although there were things I still needed to work through, God was putting people in place for me to witness to. Tashia and I instantly became close and started hanging out a lot. It was nice having a friend around who wasn't competitive and appreciated me for what I was worth.

At this point in my life, men were still approaching me, of course, but I wasn't taking anyone's mess anymore. If they came to me, they had to come correctly and respectfully. I knew my worth. Although I came with three children, my family would be a blessing to anyone who took us on.

I had to reprogram myself and gain back my true identity. I began to care how I looked again, wanting to look good for me and **ONLY** me! I wanted better for my kids and to show them the affection I never received. I settled into true motherhood—something I hadn't done from the beginning because I didn't know how to love them when I didn't love myself. I also stopped looking at all the men and their errors, while asking God to fix me. I asked Him to make me a good wife and prepare me for my husband. I adjusted my attitude, too. Although it was still there, I toned it down some. I realized every thought did not have to be voiced.

> **"The tongue has the power of life and death,
> and those who love it will eat its fruit."**
> (Proverbs 18:21)

I took a look at my situation for what it was worth. My kids were not disciplined. I had been told this before, but I ignored it. Who wants other people telling them about their kids? And truthfully, not everything others say is fact, but it doesn't hurt to listen and make a sound decision from that observance. Once my eyes were opened, I noticed my kids didn't listen and wouldn't clean up after themselves. I'm going to say it: They were downright bad!

> **"Do not withhold discipline from a child;**
> **if you punish him with the rod, he will not die."**
> (Proverbs 23:13)

My children were only learning what I taught them. I began to understand what it took to be a good mother. It wasn't enough that I kept my kids and didn't give them away as my mother did; I needed to BE their mother! It wasn't their fault that I used to be too busy partying to raise them.

I then looked at how I kept my home. I didn't dust, often left the dishes dirty, and rarely cleaned up. Everything around me was a reflection of how I felt about myself. It's so easy to point the finger at someone else. Blaming the man for all the broken relationships is easy. However, I played my part in the destruction as well. Yes, men will marry you and love your children, but you have to show them you love them first. Just as much as you don't want to sit there yelling at your bad kids, neither does he. Also, if a man is looking for a wife, he doesn't want one who doesn't clean or cook. It's just a fact: You have to do one or the other (at minimum). It's called "keeping your house in order."

Once I took a step back and truly looked at myself, I was able to start making changes. I prepared meals for my family that consisted of more than Hamburger Helper. My home-cooked meals, however, came with many trials and errors. I desired to be valuable and demonstrate to others my true worth. To do this, I had to begin loving myself more than ever. I became more responsible, independent, and most importantly, a mother. I allowed God to turn me into a Proverbs 31 Woman.

Clarity: Beauty in Pain

"A wife of noble character who can find? She is worth far more than rubies. Her husband has full confidence in her and lacks nothing of value. She brings him good, not harm, all the days of her life. She selects wool and flax and works with eager hands. She is like the merchant ships, bringing her food from afar. She gets up while it is still dark; she provides food for her family and portions for her servant girls. She considers a field and buys it; out of her earnings, she plants a vineyard. She sets about her work vigorously; her arms are strong for her tasks. She sees that her trading is profitable, and her lamp does not go out at night. In her hands, she holds the distaff and grasps the spindle with her fingers. She opens her arms to the poor and extends her hands to the needy. When it snows, she has no fear for her household; for all of them are clothed in scarlet. She makes coverings for her bed; she is clothed in fine linen and purple. Her husband is respected at the city gate, where he takes his seat among the elders of the land. She makes linen garments and sells them and supplies the merchants with sashes. She is clothed with strength and dignity; she can laugh at the days to come. She speaks with wisdom, and faithful instruction is on her tongue. She watches over the affairs of her household and does not eat the bread of idleness. Her children arise and call her blessed; her husband also, and he praises her. Many women do noble things, but you surpass them all. Charm is deceptive, and beauty fleeting; but a woman who fears the Lord is to be praised. Give her the reward she has earned, and let her works bring her praise at the city gate."
(Proverbs 31:10-31)

I began to claim my husband and was specific to God about what I wanted in a husband. I wrote down ten things, put it in my Bible, and left it there. Of course, the devil sent distractions. He sent men who made me question if "that man" was "the one." They were merely smokescreens. They presented *SOME* of the specifics I asked for in a man. That sneaky devil tried to trip me up! Understand this: God allows the devil to test us. The enemy sent a tall, dark, handsome, and successful man my way. I told him about my children, and he didn't run. He had no signs of a temper and seemed to know the Lord. However, it was tough to keep track of him. He claimed to be at work a lot and didn't have a lot of spare time. When he did have time to come over, it was late at night, and he only wanted to have sex with me. Unfortunately for **HIM**, I knew who I was and whose I was at this point.

Meanwhile, when I was bored or couldn't get a hold of "Mr. Perfect," I would get on the chat line. I didn't expect much out of it, though. Truthfully, it was all in fun. I began a conversation with a young man named Julian. He was sensitive, funny, and seemed to want to something out of his life. He had a past criminal history dating back to his youth but appeared to have redirected his life to something more positive. He didn't have the best job, but at least he had one. Oh! And he genuinely loved the Lord!

As we were getting to know each other, I decided to tell him I had three kids. Julian got quiet and told me he would call me back. Hours went by, and the phone didn't ring. I began to make all sorts of conclusions. Usually, at that point in my life, I would have just said, "Forget it! If he doesn't accept my kids, he doesn't deserve me!" Although that is my truth, I had yet to give him the opportunity to say **THAT** was the issue. I had this uncontrollable urge to call him back. I was led to put my pride aside and replace it with humility.

I called back and learned it **WASN'T** me having children that was the problem. Julian explained to me that he attempted a relationship before with a woman with children and grew attached to them. The moment they broke up or were on bad terms, she would no longer let him see the kids. He also didn't want to deal with the "baby daddy" drama. He simply didn't want to go through any of that again with anyone and would have rather avoided all the drama that could potentially come with that type of relationship. I respected him even more and told him I didn't even want him to **MEET** my kids until I thought we were going to be serious anyhow. I went on to assure him I didn't have drama as it relates to my kids and their fathers. I didn't allow it because I didn't make them think they could come back and forth in my home, to begin with.

That night, we stayed on the phone for hours, conversing about every significant detail of our lives. I felt like I was talking to a close friend I had known forever! Days turned into weeks, and before we knew it, we couldn't go without talking to each other. I took notice that "Mr. Perfect" rarely called, didn't show that he was thinking of me often, and barely wanted to spend any time with me. My choice became clear. Maturity set in and I decided that a good job, car, and house didn't mean anything if that person didn't show true feelings for me.

I learned from William that what you get in the beginning is what you will get in the end. Changing your last name doesn't change who that person is. If he was selfish, didn't communicate, or was an adulterer when you met, he will be that man after you walk down the aisle as well.

As for Julian, he wanted to spend every waking minute with me. He didn't pressure me about sex either. He would spend time with me and then return to his home, not even attempting to spend the night. When I introduced him to my mother, she immediately loved him. My mother hadn't liked anyone I brought over to meet her before. Julian was all that I asked God for and even more than I expected. He would call "just because." He put me first and always took time out to be with me. He always let me know how beautiful I was and reminded me that he was blessed to be in my presence.

This was "it"! Julian was "the one"! I just six short weeks, I was to be married to this man.

It was so obvious to me that this was the right decision. Our wedding plans flowed effortlessly. I was amazed at how it came together right before our eyes. Everyone chipped in without any arguments. My parents paid the photographer. My brother paid for the music coordination. My in-laws paid for the catering. My dress was beautiful, yet inexpensive. My maid of honors did their part, too. Without even one rehearsal, our wedding went beautifully.

As I stepped in front of that door to walk down the aisle, I wasn't even nervous. At that moment, I understood what people meant when they said, "You will just **KNOW**," because, at that very second, I just *KNEW!*

"Understand, therefore, that the Lord your God, is God; He is the faithful God, keeping His covenant of love to a thousand generations of those who love Him and keep His commandments."
(Deuteronomy 7:9)

Put It into Practice

What secret do you have that is so devastating, you don't want anyone to know about it? Does this secret torment you?

_____

_____

_____

_____

_____

_____

_____

_____

_____

_____

_____

_____

_____

_____

_____

_____

_____

Lashundra Smith

How do you feel the enemy keeps you captive with that secret?

Clarity: Beauty in Pain

Does that secret make you believe God does not love you? Seek God's Word on this and focus on the scriptures that demonstrate God's unconditional love, grace, and forgiveness.

_____
_____
_____
_____
_____
_____
_____
_____
_____
_____
_____
_____
_____
_____
_____
_____
_____
_____
_____
_____

Lashundra Smith

How can we lose God's love, grace, and mercy? Is it a gift or is it earned? If you believe it is a gift, then how can we lose it?

My Husband: Prince Charming

I had a wonderful husband, but because of the invisible walls I built up, I didn't know how to completely let him in. That is why forgiveness is so important. Without it, you can easily sabotage the next relationship. All the pains from prior relationships that had yet to be resolved resurfaced. I was taught that nothing lasts, no one is faithful, and everyone lies. Every day, as I counted each second of the first year of our marriage, I thought he was going to wake up one day, see who I really was, and walk away. Feelings of unworthiness and excess baggage clouded my judgment. Instead of seeing what my husband saw in me — that he found a beautiful wife — I saw the worst in me.

> **"He who finds a wife finds what is good and receives favor from the Lord."**
> (Proverbs 18:22)

I didn't know how to give affection as a happily-married newlywed should. I flinched when he wanted to hug, resisting his closeness. All the kissing, hugging, and cuddling hadn't been a routine part of my life. As such, I just wasn't into it. I became snappy and sarcastic, thinking that if I didn't show emotion towards Julian, it wouldn't be hard when he up and left me one day. I figured I was numb anyway and should be used to it. I didn't even know Julian noticed the walls that were encamped around my heart. I believed I put on a good show but in reality, it was noticed by more than just him.

During the Christmas holiday of our second year of marriage, we went out of town with Julian's family. I thought everything was going well. I didn't notice or feel I was nonsocial, but looking back, I realize I was. I had gotten so used to being quiet, trying to avoid saying the wrong thing or standing out in the wrong way. I protected myself by fading as much as possible into the background. At one point during the

Clarity: Beauty in Pain

trip, my mother-in-law, Lynette, called me out on it. As a true believer in Christ, she was able to discern my pain.

In so many words, Lynette told me that if I didn't learn how to love my husband and lose the brick wall, I would lose him. I was embarrassed and hurt that she said it in front of others, so I ignored the message altogether. She received a word from the Holy Spirit and felt it necessary to say it precisely when she did. I respect that. Although what she said was absolutely on the mark, it wasn't received well because of how it was presented. I am aware that she didn't mean to embarrass me, but the damage had been done at that moment.

I spent a long time focusing on **HOW** she told me instead of **WHAT** she told me. Because of that, I missed the message for a while. When I got home, sat down, and spoke to my husband, he revealed to me that he felt the disconnect between us. He didn't feel loved because I was distant towards him and sometimes downright cold. I became so accustomed to doing it, I didn't even realize it was that obvious. It hit me what was happening: I was about to lose my husband, the man who loved me past my flaws and loved my kids as if they were his own.

Julian put me through nursing school because he believed in me.

Julian fed me ice chips and rubbed my back after the birth of our child.

Julian was the man who, for the first time, stuck by me and provided my children a father figure in their young lives.

At that second, my reflecting clarified that Julian wasn't going anywhere. He had no intentions of leaving me because he loved me. If I didn't get it together, I would push him away.

I asked God to help me truly forgive everyone before him so that I could love him the way he should be loved. I began to see how much God truly loved me, to give me a man such as this. It took a very long time (approximately one year) before I was able to admit to Lynette that she was correct. God disciplines His children by His own hand or by using others.

"My son, do not despise the Lord's discipline and do not resent His rebuke, because the Lord disciplines those He loves, as a father, the son he delights in. Blessed are those who find wisdom, those who gain understanding, for she is more profitable than silver and yields better returns than rubies; nothing you desire can compare to her."
(Proverbs 3:11, 15)

I began to quietly pay attention to the way Lynette presented herself. I was in awe at the way she always gave God the glory. I grew a silent respect for her. However, the enemy did not want that relationship to develop. He didn't want me to gain some of her wisdom or her true love for Christ to be shared with me. He played every kind of mind game, convincing me she didn't like me. She would never accept my other kids because they were not kin to her. I became offended when her friends would only ask about our youngest daughter, Dee, as if I had no other children.

I felt Lynette was ashamed of our situation. I wondered how this showed me an example of God. Wouldn't a person who loves God love all my kids and forgive my past mistakes? But again, that was the enemy filling my thoughts with those lies about her. The problem wasn't her; the problem was that I needed to forgive myself for having my kids early in life. Otherwise, I probably wouldn't have even noticed or been able to point out any differences.

Finally, after a Bible study and misinterpreted conversation between Lynette and me, the devil was exposed. We both felt the other didn't want to get close to each other. I realized that all she did and said was because she **DID** love me. We both felt that neither one of us wanted to be close to each other, which was a misconception on both our parts.

If I gave her the opportunity to get to know my other kids, she could grow to love them. I thought that by keeping them away from her, I was protecting them and keeping them from being uncomfortable. Truthfully, however, I was trying to protect myself. Healing began, and I came to understand why the enemy did not want our connection to happen. He loves to create confusion and separation amongst those who love God. If he can create division amongst the believers, he can easily efeat us because we are not in agreement with each other. We are a powerful force when we come together, and the enemy can't stand that!

Lynette's presence in my life allowed for someone to advise me when I was in error. I would have someone there to tell me to trust God and not give up. Divine connections are for a reason; they create support systems.

"Though one may be overpowered, two can defend themselves. A cord of three strands is not quickly broken."
(Ecclesiastes 4:12)

After resolving several of the torn relationships in my life, I had a strong desire to meet my biological father. Sometimes, I felt I wanted a relationship with him — one that wasn't uncomfortable like the one I had with the man who raised me. At other times, I just wanted to see him out of curiosity. Did he look like me? Was his personality anything like my own? My first attempt to reach him was through Stacey. I asked her why he agreed to give me up in the first place. She explained it to me this way: "Shunda, Randall is your father's name. He had no knowledge of you. I was much younger than Randall, and he left for the Army prior to me telling him I was pregnant." She went on to say he tried to visit a few times but at that point, she had already given me away to another family and didn't know how to contact me.

When I was a bit younger and expressed interest in meeting my biological father, Stacey decided to call Randall's mother. As she began to explain my desire to meet my father, my grandmother cut her off and stated with coldness in her voice, "No. I will **NOT** tell him about her. He has a wife and kids and does not need this in his life," and then she hung up. I was truly hurt to learn that my own grandmother had no desire to not only **NOT** tell my father I was looking for him, but also that she didn't want to have anything to do with me either.

A few years later, on a second attempt to reach out to my paternal grandmother, we learned she had passed away. My heart wouldn't rest and, at 30 years of age, I decided it was necessary for me to find my biological father. I reached out to my mother, trying to get all the information on him that I could.

One Saturday, Stacey and I drove around Dallas, going to his old neighborhood and speaking to those who knew him. We found out he moved away many years ago, but his aunt — my great-aunt — had recently died, and he inherited the house right in the neighborhood. I was instantly excited and anxious at the same time, all while thinking, "Today is the day!"

We drove to his sister's house where I met my cousin. He led us to Randall's home, but to my disappointment, he wasn't there. I left him a note, detailing who I was and a phone number where he could reach me. Days and months went by. To my dismay, no contact was ever made. He is a part of me that I may always wonder about, but I know I have a Father who is more reliable than any man on earth: **GOD!** My closure would be to learn to seek *HIM* above anything or anyone else.

Marriage is not easy, even when you love each other. It takes sacrifice, compromise, and God to keep it together. It takes an agape type of love; unconditional, unwavering love that protects each other's secrets and does not neglect each other's feelings. It is indeed for better or for worse.

In our first year of marriage, we had already been through a pregnancy and birth of our youngest daughter, Deaja. Shortly after that, my husband began his trucking career while putting me through nursing school. Needless to say, the first two years were not the easiest.

I returned to school to obtain my nursing degree, and therefore, in our third year of marriage, I was a full-time student with four children at home. My husband was not a full-time truck driver and on the road for weeks at a time to provide for us. I was lonely, worried, and often felt like a single parent again. The money didn't live up to what we were told or what we expected. After gas, taxes, and constant mechanical breakdowns, we were essentially left with nothing. Thank God for Section 8 housing assistance and financial assistance with daycare expenses because we wouldn't have made it. So many times, the enemy said, "Just walk away! You could do the same thing without him!" That was a bald-faced lie! When Julian was home, I wouldn't trade the love, affection, and desire to give us the world for anything. So, we stuck it out for three years with both of us trying to deal with the separation.

Nursing school was challenging, but the experience brought friends during that season of my life that would allow us to support one another. We truly supported each other during this time, and I know that's how we all made it through. When I graduated from nursing school, I immediately advised

Section 8 that we would no longer require their assistance. I was grateful for the help, but at this point, there was no need to take advantage.

When you are afforded this rare opportunity and succeed, I believe it's time to let the assistance go for someone else to use who so desperately needs it.

After many nights of praying, my husband came home from being over the road. He looked at me and said, "I just don't want to do this anymore. I am tired of being away from my family and not even having enough to contribute to the bills. It's not worth it!" All those months of having the same conversation finally sunk in. I was so excited and felt our life was just beginning!

Little did I know the effect it would have on us in the long run.

My husband's decision to end his over-the-road career didn't go as planned. He was unable to get a local job and therefore, lost the truck. He had traded in two cars to get that truck and get his business going. It felt like it was all for nothing. He had a felony, so that didn't help matters at all. The world we live in is not as quick to forgive as God is, but in the end, God still has complete control.

Julian had been out of work for over a year. I was beginning to feel the pressure of paying all the bills. It was and has been the most difficult time for us, but even so, we are able to remain happy with each other. It did, however, send my husband into a deep depression about himself. It challenged all that we believed in. He kept condemning himself for his past decisions. He was giving up. It was not my turn to encourage my husband.

Clarity: Beauty in Pain

This was a time of struggle, pain, and confusion, but we had to be true partners to one another to keep from going around in circles, repeatedly walking in the wilderness.

"The Lord, your God, has blessed you in all the work of your hands. He has watched over your journey through this vast desert. These forty years, the Lord your God has been with you, and you have not lacked anything."
(Deuteronomy 2:7)

We were so caught up in our situation and so focused on complaining, we didn't realize God was reaching out to us.

"In the desert, the whole community grumbled against Moses and Aaron. The Israelites said to them, 'If only we had died by the Lord's hand in Egypt! There, we sat around pots of meat and ate all the food we wanted, but you have brought us out into this desert to starve this entire assembly to death.' 'You will know that it was the Lord when He gives you meat in the evening and all the bread you want in the morning because He has heard grumbling against Him. Who are we? You are not grumbling against us but against the Lord'."
(Exodus 16:2-3, 6-8)

However, we lacked nothing of necessity. Although we only had one income coming into the home, we were able to eat, be clothed, and kept a roof over our heads.

"For we brought nothing into the world, and we can take nothing out of it. But if we have food and clothing, we will be content with that. People who want to get rich fall into temptation and a trap and into many foolish and harmful desires that plunge men into ruin and destruction. For the love of money is a root of all kinds of evil. Some people, eager for money, have wandered from the faith and pierced themselves with many griefs."
(1 Timothy 6:7-10)

Everything is a test. The enemy is allowed by God to test our faith. It is at this time that God shows us what's truly in our hearts and begins to mold us into what He wants us to be. He was telling us once again that we needed Him. We could not be our best to each other without him. He let me know that the best we thought we had in each other was nothing in comparison to Him and what He had planned for us.

A lot of times when God gets tired of your mess and tired of wanting you to turn from this world to Him, He will put you in the wilderness and take away all that you know just so you will put Him first and trust Him completely with your life. When you have nothing left, you come to realize it is God who is keeping you.

During this time, we learned to seek God together. We enjoyed His presence and realized His true purpose for us on earth: to be saved so that we may go and witness to others. God wants us to be content with what we have and grateful for all that He has already blessed us with, despite our circumstances. Paul speaks of this type of gratitude to the Philippians:

"I am not saying this because I am in need, for I have learned to be content whatever the circumstances. I know what it is to be in need, and I know what it is to have plenty. I have learned the secret of being content in any and every situation, whether well-fed or hungry, whether living in plenty or in want. I can do everything through Him who gives me strength."
(Philippians 4:11-13)

"Husbands, love your wives, just as Christ loved the church and gave Himself up for her."
(Ephesians 5:25)

Put It into Practice

What do you believe in your heart makes a good husband?

Lashundra Smith

If you are unmarried, what have you done to prepare yourself for your future husband? If married, what are you doing to keep the husband you have?

Clarity: Beauty in Pain

God's Word says your husband should love you as Christ loves the church. Do you believe God would want you to have a husband who continually mistreats you?

Lashundra Smith

Decide to involve God in every aspect of your marriage. If you are not yet married, then decide to marry God today. Dress yourself up daily to impress Him, just as you would for your soon-to-be husband. Date God daily by reading His Word. Experience pleasure by being caught up in the Spirit. And curl up with Him at night with prayer. Make a note of some of your favorite passages of scripture here.

God Is a Priority, Not an Option

For several years, I remained committed to God, only to fall out of fellowship and return to the ways of the world. Each year, I participated in a women's retreat hosted by my mother-in-law for her ministry, Women of Excellence. I would leave there motivated and changed, only to walk back into the cruel world to be caught up by the enemy once again. Finally, during the fifth retreat, it took one woman to stand and share her testimony for me to realize I had yet to completely heal from all the past pains.

I thought I was healed. I thought I truly forgave those who hurt me.

As I listened to her tell her story, I realized the pain was still being harbored deep in my heart. I was still limited with my affections and unable to tell my mother I loved her when we hung up the phone. God spoke to my heart at that moment and said, "You don't know how to love." I was shocked by His rebuke and spoke back to the Holy Spirit. "Well, what have I been doing all this time?" God shocked me even more with His direct response:

"Just existing!"

Wow! I was blown away! I reflected on different occasions, noticing how fake my affections had become. My smiles were glued on, and my hugs had no warmth or feeling attached to them. I had adapted to the demands of those around me without really feeling a thing. Somehow along this journey, I became so ashamed of who I was to other people. Not only that, but I was also ashamed before God. I was led to stand and share my testimony.

As I stood, I spoke into the atmosphere, "God, I don't know how to love. Teach me how to love!" At that very moment, I was healed. All I had to do was become naked before God, and He answered.

> **"Until now, you have not asked for anything in My name. Ask, and you will receive, and your joy will be complete."**
> (John 16:24)

God not only opened my heart to love others, but also to love my husband and family in the way that I should. Affection became genuine and initiated, instead of just an obligated response.

All this time, I was unable to let the Holy Spirit in completely. Therefore, I was unable to truly be changed. God cannot enter a bitter place and rest there. How could I be a walking vessel to be used by Him if I didn't know how to love?

> **"Whoever does not love does not know God, because God is love."**
> (1 John 4:8)

Once I finally accepted love in my heart, I began to experience God on a level I never had before. I was able to truly discern God's voice from the enemy's, and my desires started to line up with His. He used me in ways I never thought I could be used before. He revealed to me the patterns in my life that caused me to fall out of fellowship with Him. I recognized that each time I stepped away from studying His Word, missed church for just a few Sundays, or shortened my prayer time with Him, I lost the cord that kept us connected. God even revealed to me that what I listened to affected me as well. If I heard club music, it made me want to go to the clubs instead of keeping my focus on Him. I learned I had to be careful what I put into my spirit because exactly those things would be what I put out.

When my eyes were fully opened, I was able to see the visible manifestations of God's goodness in my life. He showed me I was worthy to witness on His behalf, no matter my past. He revealed Himself to me the ways He had used me before, even when I didn't realize it. One amazing way God uses me is through the power of prayer. I have identified my gift to pray and intercede for myself and others.

A few years back, I met a young lady named Tarice at a job I worked for only a short period. We became fast friends and created a strong connection quickly. God moved us in different directions as far as our careers, causing us to lose touch with one another. Over the years, Tarice crossed my mind several times for reasons I couldn't understand. After all, I had many friends I lost contact with, yet they never crossed my mind again. But Tarice? She stayed on my heart so heavily, I began to pray for her. I just felt something was wrong. All I kept feeling when I thought about her was death. I didn't know if she was sick, had already passed, or what the reason was behind me feeling that way. All I knew to do was pray for her and ask God to keep her in perfect peace.

Roughly three years later, Tarice and I reconnected. Our first conversation was emotional and heartfelt. It was laid on my heart to reveal to her that I had thought of her often and prayed for her fervently over the years. She began to weep and rushed off the phone. A few weeks went by, and I started to think of her again. I had so many questions that formed in my mind.

Why was she unable to talk on the phone with me without crying?

Where was the daughter she spoke so much about?

The Holy Spirit spoke one word: "Jail!"

Now, that completely threw me for a loop. It made no sense to me at all! I texted Tarice and simply asked, "What is going on? I feel there's more to the story here. What happened to you?"

She responded, "I had been in prison for three years for aggravated assault. I began to cry when you told me you had been praying for me because so often during that time, I wanted to kill myself and be done with it. But God kept me in perfect peace and sane. He reminded me that I shall live and not die! I am still here because of people like you out here praying for me."

Tears began to flow down my face as I realized how God had used me. The Holy Spirit is with us for a reason. He led me to pray for someone I hadn't seen in years because she so desperately needed it.

When someone falls heavily on your heart, there's bound to be a reason. Stop your busy life and pray for that person! God will tell you what to say and instruct you on how to intercede for them in prayer.

What "the world" calls instinct or intuition is actually the Holy Spirit whom God has left for all of us—if we tap into God. Countless times, God has used me to pray for others. It was an obvious gift He had given me. I look back over the many times in my life and can recall the moments I began to pray, and God answered. A lot of times, I held up my own blessings because I neglected to pray, thinking something was too big or too small for God. Prayer moves mountains when you are obedient to His Word and have faith, believing in what you have asked Him for.

"If you believe, you will receive whatever you ask for in prayer."
(Matthew 21:22).

Recently, my sister Sheila was very ill. She had been battling with the disease, Lupus, for over 25 years. It appeared as though the disease had finally taken over. Both of her kidneys had failed, and she was on dialysis three times a week. After several surgeries and constant infections, she became deathly ill. She was unresponsive. All her veins had collapsed, so they had nowhere to put an intravenous line. Her inability to control her movements forced her to pull out the feeding tube in her nose, causing her to be too weak for surgery and unable to receive pain medications. The doctor instructed my mother to gather the family, and the nurse advised me that even if Sheila came out of it, she would be in a vegetative state. At this point, my mother was making funeral arrangements.

I decided that if man could do nothing else for her, I knew someone who could. I called on the **ULTIMATE** healer: **GOD!** I requested other prayer warriors to join in and asked that we all pray at a specific time for my sister's healing. By 8:00 a.m. the next morning, my mother received a call from the hospital. The nurse handed the phone to Sheila, and she spoke to my mother as if nothing ever happened!

You see, it's not over until **GOD** says it's over! God is faithful! He is still in the miracle-working business. The miracles He did a hundred years ago, He is still able to do now. He is the **SAME** God who raised Lazarus from the dead many years ago, as recorded in John 11:17-44:

"On His arrival, Jesus found that Lazarus had already been in the tomb for four days. Now, Bethany was less than two miles from Jerusalem, and many Jews had come to Martha and Mary to comfort them in the loss of their brother. When Martha heard that Jesus was coming, she went out to meet Him, but Mary stayed at home. 'Lord,' Martha said to Jesus, 'if you had been here, my brother would not have died. But I know that even now, God will give You whatever You ask.' Jesus said to her, 'Your brother will rise

Clarity: Beauty in Pain

again.' Martha answered, 'I know he will rise again in the resurrection at the last day.' Jesus said to her, 'I am the resurrection and the life. The one who believes in Me will live, even though they die; and whoever lives by believing in Me will never die. Do you believe this?' 'Yes, Lord,' she replied, 'I believe that You are the Messiah, the Son of God, who is to come into the world.' After she had said this, she went back and called her sister Mary aside. 'The Teacher is here,' she said, 'and is asking for you.' When Mary heard this, she got up quickly and went to Him. Now, Jesus had not yet entered the village but was still at the place where Martha had met Him. When the Jews who had been with Mary in the house, comforting her, noticed how quickly she got up and went out, they followed her, supposing she was going to the tomb to mourn there. When Mary reached the place where Jesus was and saw Him, she fell at His feet and said, 'Lord, if You had been here, my brother would not have died.' When Jesus saw her weeping, and the Jews who had come along with her also weeping, He was deeply moved in spirit and troubled. 'Where have you laid him?' He asked. 'Come and see, Lord,' they replied. Jesus wept. Then, the Jews said, 'See how He loved Him!' But some of them said, "Could not He who opened the eyes of the blind man have kept this man from dying?' Jesus, once more deeply moved, came to the tomb. It was a cave with a stone laid across the entrance. 'Take away the stone,' He said. 'But Lord,' said Martha, the sister of the dead man, 'by this time, there is a bad odor, for he has been there four days.' Then, Jesus said, 'Did I not tell you that if you believe, you will see the glory of God?' So, they took away the stone. Then Jesus looked up and said, 'Father, I thank You that You have heard me. I know that You always hear Me, but I said this for the benefit of the people standing here, that they may believe that You sent Me.' When He had said this, Jesus called in a loud voice, 'Lazarus, come out!' The dead man came out, his hands and feet wrapped with strips of linen and a cloth around his face. Jesus said to them, 'Take off the grave clothes and let him go.'"

As I began to change, my whole family began to change as well. It only takes one! Although it may not seem fair, someone has to do it. Someone has to break the cycle. You may ask yourself, "Why **ME**?" However, God is asking, "Why **NOT** you?" Consider yourself worthy to be used by such a mighty God. If it takes you being an example to change another's life, then do it. Be naked and not ashamed because someone out there is waiting for your testimony to bring them healing. Pain does not discriminate. Every one of us has been hurt in some way. Revealing yourself to others not only helps heal them but it also, in turn, heals you.

I am now healed just for writing this book and being transparent before you.

I have realized that my life and testimony are not for me. My testimony is required to witness to someone else who needs the wisdom God has granted me through my experiences. It was then I realized why God brought my friend Tashia into my life. She was there so that I could witness to her. I saw in her some of the same mistakes I made and understood it was time to share with her my testimony. I took the time to explain to her that the strong person she saw before her today was not always this way. I struggled with insecurities, promiscuity, and not knowing God as I should—just as she did. At first, I believed it was going in one ear and out the other. It appeared as though she hadn't heard a word I said. I almost gave up, but God reminded me He never gave up on me.

After many conversations with Tashia, it was time to practice tough love. She and I began working together last year. At the same time, she started dating one of my husband's friends, John. That same weekend, they had sex. The following week, he dumped her. John told us that a friend of his saw her picture in his phone and stated, "I smashed [had sex] with her before, and she gets around." I thought back to how often that

Clarity: Beauty in Pain

happened to her and recognized the pattern. My spirit wouldn't rest. It was time for a serious tough love conversation.

As we were heading home one day, I began to minister to her. It was the most difficult conversation I had to have. I explained to her that the way men treated her could no longer be blamed on them and that the mistreatment was on her. As long as she treated herself and body like trash, that is how she would be treated; used and thrown away.

As expected, Tashia began to cry as I continued to speak to her about the way she presented herself. At first, she was defensive, stating that the rumors or things I heard were untrue. I looked at her, and with all the courage I could muster up, called her out on the behavior I had seen with my own eyes.

"You have dated brothers and had sex with both of them. You have also met many men and had sex with them the same day. Does this not confirm the rumors being spread about you? It doesn't matter if what the guy told John is the truth or not because you have already exhibited behaviors that confirm what he says."

I didn't want to say that, but I tried to talk to her in other ways, hinting around at what was happening around her, and she never received it.

As I ministered to her, I didn't just sit there pointing my finger while identifying all the bad. I sat with her and watched as the tears rolled down her face. She was listening to what I said. I told her to look at me and then spoke from my heart: "You are beautiful. Do you know that?" She didn't speak, so I continued to talk. "If you don't know you are beautiful, no one else will. You have to know this for yourself."

After our talk, I got out of the car, not knowing if I even had a friend anymore. Still, I knew I did what was right.

Well, our friendship didn't end. In fact, I think we became closer! She respected my honesty and God began to change her. He used me and all my past situations to relate and minister to someone else. I truly understood what I was on this earth for. My tragedies were not for me, but others. God wanted to use me—if I let Him!

God was revealing to me through others the importance of being available to Him. He uses us here on earth to say the right words or exhibit the right behaviors to save a soul. He was showing my husband and I that things we thought were important were irrelevant. Life is not about the material things of this world or even the people in it.

"Since, then, you have been raised with Christ, set your hearts on things above, where Christ is seated at the right hand of God. Set your minds on things above, not on earthly things. For you died, and your life is now hidden with Christ in God. When Christ, who is your life, appears, then you also will appear with Him."
(Colossians 3:4)

Friends come and go and can even be taken away, but God's grace and mercy are new every day. When you truly begin to seek Him, it is then that you find peace and prosperity.

The decision to follow Christ was not without tests. When you are walking with the enemy, he will lead you to believe life is all good. When you are experiencing life and notice you have no problems physically, but emotionally you are dried up, you are usually already on the enemy's side. When you decide to change teams, the devil realizes he has lost control and becomes enraged. Then, his attacks begin on your life to cause confusion and make you believe that following

Clarity: Beauty in Pain

Christ is not the way to go. He will continuously make you believe that when you were following him, life was good when, in fact, it wasn't. You were on a straight road to Hell. You had no joy, and when a problem arose, you had no idea how to deal with it. Choosing to follow God is a conscious decision to serve Him and gain eternity in His presence.

Once you decide to join the winning team, God will allow the enemy to test you. He wants to make sure you are the faithful servant you claim to be and that His grace is sufficient for thee.

"Be joyful in hope, patient in affliction, and faithful in prayer."
(Romans 12:12)

When my husband and I decided to follow Christ, that was when the devil raised his ugly head. It became a domino effect of attacks in our lives. My husband remained unemployed. Although he filled out applications daily, he was rejected at every turn. His manhood was repeatedly tested as well. This created a heavier weight on my shoulders, which neither of us wanted on them. My husband was doing all he knew to do and helped in the house in ways I appreciated. However, it didn't stop our pain or our struggles.

Time progressed, and it seemed like we were getting our heads above water. We continued to pray and seek God in our daily lives. We had been hoping to find a home and get out of our apartment and received a number to a credit repair guy. His name was Jason. He seemed to be a very fair young man and made us promises we were sure he would keep. Jason introduced us to a mortgage company that would work to help us get a home.

After paying Jason $500.00 for the repairs to our credit and waiting patiently for the results, three months later we were told we were in a position to purchase. Like clockwork, we received credit reports weekly with deletions, so I trusted the work had been done. We contacted the mortgage company, and they preapproved the loan. We found a builder and put up $1,000.00 in hard-earned money, and another $800.00 as a deposit for upgrades.

Before knowing we were getting a home, I put down a $500.00 deposit on a trip to the Bahamas. I felt canceling the trip and forfeiting the deposit was a sound decision so that we could put the extra money we would have spent on the trip into the house.

Weeks went by. Soon, the foundation to our new home was laid and getting the house became a reality…until reality returned to fantasy. The mortgage company told us our scores had not gone up as promised and that they were nowhere near where they needed to be to purchase a home.

We had been swindled out of our money.

With a total of $2,800.00 gone, we were no closer to getting a home than when we first met "Jason the Swindler." I was devastated, disappointed, confused, and angry yet again. The enemy instantly said to me, "See? You did all that trusting, believing, and praying for no reason." But my **GOD** said, "Call Lynette."

To God be the glory for the family. Lynette was sad for us but told me with tough love, "It's okay to be sad and even disappointed, but you cannot stay in a pity party about it. The devil comes to steal, kill, and destroy. His purpose is to steal your joy. Don't allow him to do it!" She reminded me that what the devil means for bad, God will turn it around for my good.

Clarity: Beauty in Pain

You see, although we wanted the home, we were not ready. God knew this better than us. I felt I could carry the bulk of the load on my income, but God knew the mortgage payment they were expecting would be too much for me to handle. Even though God said "Not now," He didn't say "Not ever!" It was most important for me to trust Him now more than ever. He would return what I lost seven times over. Vengeance was His!

"Do not take revenge, my friends, but leave room for God's wrath, for it is written, 'It is Mine to avenge; I will repay,' says the Lord." (Romans 12:19).

I remembered to praise God through my circumstances and felt some relief. All the money we put into the house caused us to struggle. We basically paid two mortgage payments in one month. We double our utility bills by trying to invest in the home and keep our bills paid. We went weeks without food in the refrigerator. Still, God always made sure we ate. Somehow, I didn't worry as much as I usually did.

"Therefore, I tell you; do not worry about your life, what will you eat or drink, or about your body, what you will wear. Is not life more important than clothes? Look at the birds of the air. They do not sow or reap or store away in barns, and yet your Heavenly Father feeds them. Are you much more valuable than they?" (Matthew 6:25-26).

I trusted God and was **NOT** going to let the enemy break me. Yet, as long as we are here on this earth, the enemy will not stop trying. So, it wasn't long before the next attack came.

The next time I got paid, I was able to pay several bills and purchase money orders for the ones I wasn't able to pay online. I felt I could breathe again! On my way to work the next morning, I was pulled over by the police. The car insurance had lapsed a few days prior, and I was just about to drop the payment in the mail. I lowered my head to the steering wheel and thought, "God! Give me a break!" I had warrants from five years ago **AND** no car insurance. I knew I was going to jail, so I called my husband. He was asleep and didn't answer the phone. I was frustrated to the max!

I kept thinking, "Lord knows I haven't had the money to pay the tickets with one income in the home (the tickets were for someone else's kids riding in my car without a seat belt)." I was taken to jail with no bond because I neglected previous payment arrangements. To top it off, my car was being towed. I couldn't help feeling sorry for myself and wondering how on earth I was going to come up with $961.00 **PLUS** the amount to get my car out of the pound. My husband ended up cashing in all the money orders we had purchased to pay bills to get me out of jail so that I could return to work before I lost my job.

The devil was trying his hardest to break me. He wanted me to give up. He wanted me to stop praising God, reading His Word, and praying. I must admit: I was so tired of what seemed like repeated failures. I went and sat in my car in the garage with the lights out, just to get away from my frustrations. I also didn't want my husband to find out how emotionally drained I was. He was already blaming himself for everything we were going through.

All the while, the enemy was on his job, reminding me of how it used to be and that life was never **THIS** bad before! He taunted, "Just go back to the old ways! Just give up! It's pointless!" But through it all, I could hear *GOD* speak. HE kept saying, "I love you. No matter what happens, remember that I love you. No matter what you don't have, no matter what you lose, you still have My unconditional love. Is that enough?

Clarity: Beauty in Pain

A moment of clarity and wisdom was given to me at that moment in the car:

> "Be self-controlled and alert. Your enemy, the devil, prowls around like a roaring lion, looking for someone to devour. Resist him, standing firm in the faith, because you know that your brothers throughout the world are undergoing the same kind of sufferings."
> (1 Peter 5:8-9)

I came to understand how the enemy worked. The many times my husband and I tried to follow God and didn't succeed were clear. The times we kept backsliding were because we let the devil confuse us. For some, they turn to Christ and never look back; for many others, this is not the case. It takes time for a change. It doesn't happen overnight. Sometimes, it takes failures and getting knocked down to get back up again. Sometimes, it takes God to knock you so low, you can't look up to anyone but Him.

When I returned to work, to my surprise, my company was completely supportive of me. Not only did they not condemn me for going to jail, but they also gave me an advance so that my family could survive until my next check! I was able to see who my true friends were who were there for me. A dear friend of mine from work even gave us a $50.00 gift card to Wal-Mart for food. God was showing me once more that He was there for us, no matter what the enemy tried to tell me. As a reward for my faithfulness, I was able to drive without having to look over my shoulder. The warrants that chased me were now behind me. God was getting rid of all the old stuff so that He could introduce me to my new beginnings.

The desire to hold onto the things of this world was no more. I was no longer happy with "just existing" without God. I wanted to be in God's presence, and nothing else could make me feel like He did. I desired His Word daily, and my purpose was made clear: to serve Him—not man, not idols, just Him. Slowly, my prayers became unselfish and were more about others. Instead of praying about money and material things, I prayed to be humble and to forgive, even when I didn't feel like it. The chains of bondage were being set free!

I wanted my kids to know God better, learn how to pray, and be guided by Him and no one else. I wanted the curses on my family broken, and it started with me. I began to pray for my husband like never before. I watched as God changed him day by day. I started attending church with or without him. I began letting God use me and started teaching in the Children's ministry at my church. I noticed all the positive things life had to offer instead of focusing on the negative. I praised God and thanked Him, even when He said no to something I really wanted. I trusted that He knew what He was doing and that nothing He did was to hurt me.

"For I know the plans I have for you," declares the Lord, "
plans to prosper you and not to harm you,
plans to give you hope and a future."
(Jeremiah 29:11)

We realized how important church was and made every effort to find a true church home with motives to please God. However, we should not get caught up in a man wherever we decide to plant our feet. No one is always going to be there for you outside of God, so the point of going to church is to get the right teachings, be fed by the Word, and grow from it. It is not necessary to know the pastor on a personal level, but it IS necessary to pay attention to his motives. The Word of God is most important. Even if the pastor doesn't know you by name or personally sit down and talk with you, discern how he is leading his flock. Is it by the Word of God alone?

If you are not getting a good word and you leave the church the same each time, you are not planted in fertile ground. If you are making decisions about not being in a good church home based on its size, then you are making a huge mistake. You knowing the pastor on a personal level will not get you into Heaven. When Jesus walked the earth, every man did not meet Him. Every man did not have the opportunity to touch Him. He did not attend every funeral or wedding, but His teachings lived on nonetheless. And He died for each person born of sin into this world without touching each one of them physically with His hands. He left us with the Bible — His Word and instruction — that will, in the end, touch each of our hearts.

Slowly, my desires were replaced with what God wanted for me and not what I wanted. I began to submit to Him and not myself. God began to bless my family in so many ways. My husband just keeps getting better each day. I keep falling in love with him repeatedly. I am now a Children's Ministry Leader at my church. My children have become more precious to me than I could have ever imagined not so long ago. I long to stay connected with all of my family, both immediate and extended.

Life became real to me, and my eyes were wide open to what I had been missing. I even reached back out to Jaleesa and Teisha, the sisters I missed so much who were truly (when I sat back and thought about it) my best friends. Although we went through a lot, we did love one another. We understood each other and were able to put the past in the past. I wanted our children to have the opportunity to be blessed by the relationship we created years ago.

Are you ready for the **NEXT** testimony? Here goes:

In August 2010, God blessed my family with the home we wanted, not even two months after we lost the house we were going to have built! The house was less expensive but came with all the upgrades we originally wanted. Also, we didn't have to come up with all the money we were going to need to invest in the other house. The government ended up owing me $2,700.00, and we received it just in time to move into our new home, allowing us to decorate with **NEW** furniture. I was reminded of my prayers at work each morning before all the trials began. I asked God to allow us to move into a home before the end of August, with little or no money, *AND* the funds to buy new furniture. God answered my prayers!

When you are specific, God is specific in His response. The first house was not what I asked God for, and God is not a man that He shall lie (Numbers 23:19).

Just this past March, Julian was blessed with a job. It's not just any job, but one with the possibility of making six figures. God did not intend to hurt us by sitting Julian down for over a year, but rather to groom us for what He had planned for us. The year and a half Julian hadn't worked taught us patience, love, and undeniable strength. We have learned our marriage can withstand any test if we keep God as the head of our household.

We began to depend on God and have true faith in His Word. We gained so much from that struggle. Money could never pay for the lessons we learned during that time. We now know that whatever God has planned will happen according to His will and not our own. He is faithful to those who believe!

Journey to Peace

Although I'd finally found my Prince Charming, life continued to hit me with significant setbacks. My sister Sheila died in 2011 after her fight with Lupus, and then my brother Steve passed away in 2014. The loss of two siblings weighed heavily on me.

I went into this phase where I acknowledged that life is short and I needed to forgive any and everyone. I began to question myself again and found myself in the cycle of choosing friendships that were unhealthy for me. Those past feelings of rejection resurfaced, causing me to chase relationships once again. I was so lonely at one point, I went online seeking friendships.

You can never make sound decisions when made out of desperation.

I had a habit of choosing those unavailable to me which, in turn, caused me to chase them more. I was selecting friends I had nothing in common with. They had no relationship with God, lacked self-worth, and were unreliable. Loyalty was dependent upon what I gave to the relationship and, if I pulled back at all, I heard from no one. I was in a place of loneliness, yet I had a host of friends. For years, I remained in this lonely state. I repeatedly complained to my husband about those "friends," yet I tried to hold onto the friendships even though I didn't feel fulfilled in them. I needed to understand (once again) that my fulfillment comes from my continuous relationship with God.

> **"A man of many companions may come to ruin, but there is a friend who sticks closer than a brother."**
> (Proverbs 18:24)

Then, on January 16, 2018, my father, Sammie Harris, Jr. passed away after a two-year battle with cancer. Although it was a two-year battle for him, he hid his suffering from us until the very end. He was adamant that al the family needed to be together during what would be our last Thanksgiving holiday with him. We didn't understand the urgency at the time because he told us he was in remission. Little did we know that the doctor had already given him eight months to live several months prior. When he passed away, it was a shock to us because we truly thought he was going to be okay, at least for a while longer.

The loss of my father opened my eyes to what was important: my peace. I had to sit back and reevaluate my friendships because when he passed, I looked around for them, and no one was there. Yes, I received a text message or Facebook comment, but no one was **REALLY** there for me. No knock on the door. No repeated check-in calls. I was left alone to grieve with the rest of my family. To make matters worse, my mom took it harder than we could have ever imagined.

When I say it was a shock to us, it in no way compares to the effect his passing had on her. See, my father died in his wheelchair at his bank. My mother told the story once and **ONLY** once the day he died because afterward, she was never the same again. Sitting next to my father's body at the hospital, my mother told his story. She said my father had been begging her for days to take him to the bank. The dialogue between the two of them went something like this:

Mom: "Sammie, we are not going to the bank. It's freezing outside, and you are so weak, you can't even walk."

Dad: "I *SAID* take me to the bank, woman!" Mom said that he said it with such force that last day, she called on my brother and nephew to help get him in the van.

When they arrived at the bank, he weakly explained to the clerk that he needed all of his accounts transferred to my mom immediately. When the teller asked for his confirmation, he was grabbing at his chest as he nodded his head yes. The teller stated, "Mr. Harris, I realize you are too weak to speak, but if you nod your head again, I can make this happen for you." As my father nodded his head again, his heart stopped, and he died right there at the teller's counter.

The paramedics said it took all of them to pull my mom off of my dad as she screamed, **"HE BETTER NOT BE DEAD!"**

As my mom ended her story, she looked at me and said, "I am so angry with your father for leaving me here. How could he do this? Fifty-six years of marriage, and now he is gone. It isn't fair! I've had to bury two of my kids and now, my husband." I don't think I ever felt that much pain for another person in my life as I felt at that moment.

That was the last time I had a normal conversation with my mom. By the time we had the funeral, she had checked out mentally. The stress and pain from the loss of my dad somehow catapulted her into full-blown Alzheimer's. A woman who had just cooked a full Thanksgiving dinner, still cared for her home, and advised and encouraged me was no longer able to walk, talk in complete sentences, or remember her kids.

Her sadness turned into physical illness. She had multiple strokes, with the doctors unable to control her blood pressure or blood sugar. After weeks of rehab and no progress, she was discharged to go back home. During this time, unbeknownst to us, my sister had gotten power of attorney over mom. My older brother and sister were now in control, leaving me to feel like the outcast. Not feeling like a member of the family hadn't hit me in a long time because my mother made it her mission to ensure I no longer felt that way, but the woman she was to me was gone.

This season of turmoil continued to grow into something I never saw coming. As my mother went in and out of the hospital, we received a call from the children's school with some devastating news. Something happened to one of our kids by my nephew, the son to that same sister with the power of attorney. It is not my story to tell here. I will allow that child to tell their story when they are ready, but I will say this: The incident revealed to us the state our family was really in.

The family I was raised with since I was three months old turned their backs on me. Accusations of lies and setups were used to explain the tragic situation instead of facing reality. I tried to put myself in my sister's shoes and understand she was only protecting her child, but in doing so, there was no sympathy for mine. I prayed to God to convict them, yet show them mercy.

> **"Bless those who curse you,**
> **and pray for those who mistreat you."**
> (Luke 6:28).

In May 2018, I received a dreadful call: My mother had a terrible stroke and was unresponsive. She was put on life support to be monitored and see if she would return to us. A week passed, and we were informed there was no brain activity and that if she did come back, she would be in a vegetative state. We had to decide to pull the plug. That same sister and I sat in the room with my mother and watched as she took labored breaths. My brother was hysterically yelling at our mom saying that he wouldn't make it in this world without her. I stopped him and told him he was extremely selfish! Although the doctors said our mother couldn't hear us or understand anything we spoke, I felt her spirit there. I whispered in my mother's ear, "If you want to go and be with daddy, Steve, and Sheila, momma, you can go. You were and will always be the best mom ever. Your job is done. We will be okay." One tear slid down my mother's face. Until this very day, I believe she heard me. It took three days after being disconnected from life support for our mother to die.

On May 9, 2018—less than four months after my dad passed—God called my mother home. Before burying her, my brother revealed to me that our dad had saved a hundred thousand dollars that would be split among us. There were also three cars to split between the three of us, one of which was promised to my daughter. I was told I would receive a call about a week after the funeral to discuss those arrangements. I never got that call. Instead of giving my daughter the car she was promised, it was given to my brother's estranged wife. Shortly after, my nephew was arrested for what he did, and therefore, I never heard from my sister again. Until this day, I still don't know what happened to my portion of the inheritance.

My brother was living on the land and in the house my parents worked so hard for and began to leave threatening messages on my voicemail. He called me out my name and told me never to show my face at my mother's house again. He actually said he hoped God did something horrible to my family and me for getting justice for our child.

Again, I prayed for mercy for them. Despite the pain inflicted, I felt the prayer was necessary. They had no idea what doing something like "that" to a child of God would do. I had to grieve the loss of not only both parents but now the loss of the only family I'd known. A few months later, my brother was thrown back in jail as a three-time offender. He will likely never see the free world again.

Clarity: Beauty in Pain

> **"Do not take revenge, my dear friends,
> but leave room for God's wrath, for it is written,
> 'Vengeance is Mine, I will repay,' says the Lord.'**
> (Romans 12:19)

I had reached rock bottom and was in that place of sadness, confusion, and loneliness all over again. I had lost both parents—and where were my friends? I was even yelled at for not telling one "friend" about the passing of my mom the way they wanted, causing our "friendship" to be severed the day after I buried my mother. However, I am grateful for that moment because I realized who people were to me and made a decision to put myself first. I no longer reached out to people. That wasn't my job during this difficult time; it was theirs. I stopped seeking attention from those I had to chase. If they didn't call me during this time, I moved on.

I began to pray like never before! I relied on past experiences and the understanding that God was and is the same God yesterday, today, and forever. I knew the pain was here now, but in time, it would fade. I trusted in that. It's like this shield over my eyes had been lifted, and I could see clearly. I started to pay attention to who was there: my husband and kids. Much to my surprise, my sister Jaleesa was also there the whole time. When my father died, she was at my side. When my mom died, she called, texted, and visited to make sure I was okay. She didn't rely on my social media posts but rather the communication between her and me. Our relationship evolved, and we began to talk daily. Next thing I knew, we were best friends again!

We recognized why the enemy fought so hard to keep us apart. Together, we had something the world needed, and he was intentional about keeping confusion going on between the two of us. Now, we communicate often and are closer than ever.

As crazy as it sounds, the loss of my parents brought me peace in areas I struggled with for so long. My "self-love" went through the roof. I no longer accepted mediocre relationships. If the effort was not made, I didn't make any either. If invitations were repeatedly flaked on or not given, I just stopped inviting them. There was no longer stress about having friends. I simply no longer cared! If it didn't bring me peace, I didn't need or want it around me. I felt I had so much drama in my life already that I had reached a point where I wasn't accepting any more slack. When they say that life is too short, they meant it! It's too short to be in constant chaos and turmoil with yourself or others. Sometimes, you have to cut even your family off if they're not bringing you peace.

Put It into Practice

What has chasing material things gotten you thus far? How long do they last when you take your focus off of God?

_____
_____
_____
_____
_____
_____
_____
_____
_____
_____
_____
_____
_____
_____
_____
_____
_____
_____

Lashundra Smith

Do you consider yourself wealthy? If you consider yourself poor, ask yourself this question: Do I eat daily, have my health and strength, have clothes on my back, and a place to eat? I ask again: Are you wealthy?

Clarity: Beauty in Pain

*Is there anyone or anything you can truly say has **NEVER** let you down? Has God ever let you down? List a memorable moment when God showed up in a mighty way on your behalf.*

Lashundra Smith

Clarity: Beauty in Pain

Miracles Still Happen

After what most would consider a horrible year, I began to heal on the inside. I was able to remember my parents with fondness, and although we are currently in court behind our children, I have already forgiven them. I understand the battle was not mine; it's the Lord's (2 Chronicles 20:15)!

As I began to heal, God began to grow me in ways I could not have imagined. He began to use me by doing videos to speak to women about things I had gone through. In doing those videos and initiating a YouTube channel with my sister, I realized I was missing the calling on my life.

One Friday, as I sat in front of my computer, God gave me the name "Women with Balance." In one weekend, I purchased the domain, built the website, and created an entire clothing line for the ministry. Everything fell right into place—even the fact that the name was available on **ALL** social media platforms! The decision to be obedient not only catapulted me into my destiny, but my husband began photography to assist me in the endeavor. He ended up not only loving it but is also amazing with his art!

As God began to stir up those gifts, new businesses were developed. My mind was no longer occupied with sadness and grief. However, as I embarked on this new venture, something was still missing. After years of not really thinking about it (because I had pushed it to the back of my subconscious), I realized I still desired to know my biological father. The week of Thanksgiving 2018, those thoughts weighed heavily on my mind due, in part, to the holidays being a time to be with family. With mine being gone, I felt alone. I shook off the emotion, though, and made it through the week.

The following week, however, I became gravely ill with the flu which, in turn, became bronchitis. I was home from work for two weeks completely idle. To say it mildly, I was bored. I was sitting in front of my computer attempting to work from home and thoughts of my father began to creep in again. At that moment, it was as if I heard someone whisper, *"Just Google him."* I thought to myself, *"For **WHAT**? That's like trying to find a needle in a haystack!"* All my mom ever told me was his name, the high school he attended, and the area in which he grew up, but that was 39 years ago.

Once I moved past all the questions in my head, I decided to follow the instruction of that voice. After all, why not? What did I have to lose? I entered his name in the search engine. Several matches came up, so I started the process of elimination based on age and location. Once I completed that task, I was left with only one that matched his profile. I took a deep breath and dialed the number, totally expecting he wouldn't answer. I was prepared to leave a voicemail, but to my surprise, he answered the phone!

Me: "Hi. Is this Robert?"

Robert: "Yes, this is he. How can I help you?"

Me: "Uh… This is awkward, but it's very possible I am your daughter."

Robert: "No. I don't have any other kids."

Me: "Well, I think you do."

I then shared with him what I knew. My mother lost her virginity to him, and shortly after, he left for the Army. I attempted to explain who my mother was and he stated he did not remember her. However, once I told him things about himself, he knew I somehow knew him. He kept listening. Initially, he didn't think it made sense to even bother building a relationship this late in life. When he hung up the phone after that call, I thought I would never hear from him again. I was completely prepared to give up, but then, I began to pray. I asked God to please open Robert's heart.

The next morning, Robert called me. He said he wanted to meet me! He and his fiancé met me at a deli across from my home. I then told him my story. It was uncanny looking at him. It was like looking in a mirror! For so many years, I felt I didn't really look like anyone in my family. My siblings looked like their dad, leaving me always to feel left out…the "odd" one. Seeing Robert made me feel like I finally belonged to someone! He was so warm and accepting. He was shocked but definitely receptive. I needed that.

When I broke the news to my mom that I had met my father and were preparing to take a DNA test, she hit me with a blow that knocked the wind out of me. The paternity was in questions for reasons out of her control (it's not my story to tell here), but her response sent me into a tailspin of depression and hopelessness. I thought my happiness was within reach and just as fast, it may be gone. Even though I tried to lose hope that Robert was my father in order to protect myself, hope remained. For days, I didn't sleep and could barely eat as we waited on the DNA results. The devil kept telling me that Robert was not my father. In my heart, I believed he was.

I finally received notification that the results were back. Although it felt like an eternity had passed, it had only been three days. The email notification popped up, causing my heart to race uncontrollably. I was so scared to open it, fearing the worst.

The test proved without a doubt that Robert was my father! Just like that, I now have another dad!

We were both overjoyed by the news! Our bond was instant and unexplainable. It's like our genetic makeup just **KNEW**! Prior to the results, I felt a connection with him that I can't put into words.

So, right before Christmas, after losing both my parents, siblings who no longer wanted anything to do with me, and a host of other relationships lost, I had a new family to get to know and love. It felt like my parents sent me this gift, letting me know they didn't leave me alone on this earth.

God's timing is **ALWAYS** good. It's perfection at its best. It's never when we think, but rather when *HE* knows best. Once God is made a priority in your life, He brings the right people to you.

I no longer desire or maintain unhealthy, toxic relationships. I released those who meant me no good or were negative and discouraging. Those are not real friends. I've made my circle smaller, focusing on those who take the time out to invite me places, think of me, and encourage me.

A friend will drop what she is doing to support you. She will listen when you need to vent and give good, sound advice regarding your situation. A true friend is happy for you, even when you don't know how to be happy for yourself. A true friend includes you in her life effortlessly because she wants you there. A true friend knows when they have hurt you and is willing to apologize to you for what they have done or attempt to correct whatever the circumstance.

If you constantly have to invite yourself to spend time with a friend or reach out to them, that is not a friend. If you are always giving and giving and that person just takes and never gives back, that is not a friend either.

However, it is imperative that we be in a position to receive those positive people into our lives. God must be first, and we have to love ourselves to get and keep a friend like that. It took me a long time to have that type of friendship because I didn't know how to be a friend myself. It's not always the other person's fault. A lot of times, we have to do a self-evaluation and check ourselves when we are missing something in our lives.

Some things may not be major to the rest of the world but are very significant to God. He wants to be first in our lives, no matter what. Even though we will still mess up from time to time, God wants us to look to Him first. That is the only way to grow personally and achieve the things He has planned for us. God does not want us to suffer, but if that's what it takes for us to recognize that He is God, He will allow it. Most importantly, God wants us to respect and love one another. If we borrow something, at least attempt to give it back.

> **"The wicked borrows and does not pay back,
> but the righteous is gracious and gives."**
> (Psalms 37:1)

If you cause another pain, apologize. Once you have apologized, the other person has to answer to God for their unforgiveness. Pray for one another without waiting to be asked. Love your neighbors, especially if you claim to love the Lord. People are watching your behavior and what you do can affect how they feel about the Christian life.

After truly learning to trust God, He began to change my way of thinking. The things I used to get upset about didn't aggravate me anymore. I am now able to look at life from a different perspective. If I am late for work, I thank God for whatever I may have avoided, such as a car accident. If He takes something from me, I know it is to protect me and not to hurt me. If people leave my life, it is for my good and theirs. God will not allow those He has chosen to hold onto anything that keeps them from Him.

Through it all, God often reminded me that I shall live and not die! He forgave me when I continually denied Him and His power. He loved me when I didn't even love myself. When I finally decided to call on His name, He healed my old wounds and saved me.

> "Heal me, O Lord, and I will be healed; save me, and I will be saved, for You are the one I praise."
> (Jeremiah 17:14)

He carried me when I was walking through life in a daze.

> "When I said, 'My foot is slipping,' Your unfailing love, LORD, supported me. When anxiety was great within me, Your consolation brought me joy."
> (Psalms 94:18-19)

> "But seek first His kingdom and His righteousness, and all these things will be given to you as well."
> (Matthew 6:33)

God **IS** Alpha and Omega, The Beginning and The End!

Lashundra Smith

Epilogue

I encourage you to look over your own life and remember the worst of times. Yes, the worst. Those times you felt like depression was weighing you down, and you had no more fight to give. Then, the next day came, and you were able to breathe again. Recall the time you lost your job and was left with no income, yet you never went without a necessity. Remember that time your car broke down, but you still made it to work each day. Remember the time you made a mistake, went to prison, and thought you would lose your mind, but you were granted not only a second chance but also maintained your sanity. Lastly, think about the time you were told you had cancer. You wanted to give up, but something kept tugging at your heart not to give in and to fight! Now, you are cancer free!

All those times, Jesus was watching you, keeping you, and carrying you through it all. He made a way out of no way. He had someone give you money you weren't expecting. He gave you strength you had no idea you possessed. Contrary to popular belief, nothing in life is a coincidence, but rather divine timing that God had set for you before you came from your mother's womb. He knew the day you would be hungry and need food. He knew the day you would have to raise your kids alone. He even knew the very day you would have to deal with the death of a loved one. The grief was so unbearable, you couldn't get out the bed each morning, but God pushed you each day to go on.

God allows these hardships to happen in our lives so that we will recognize who is carrying us: **HIM!** His Word verifies this in Ecclesiastes 7:14:

"When times are good, be happy; but when times are bad, consider this: God has made the one as well as the other. Therefore, a man cannot discover anything about his future."

Looking back at these times, we have no choice but to recognize His holy existence and know that He alone is God.

Maybe you didn't recognize Him before. Perhaps you thought it was just a coincidence, but now your heart knows who was keeping you all this time. It's not too late to thank Him! You can ask Him right now to come into your heart and show you the way.

"For everyone who calls on the name of the Lord will be saved."
(Romans 10:13)

This is only the beginning of your walk with Him. He will lead you, guide you, and direct you. No, it won't be easy, but He has left His biography—the Holy Bible—so that you may get to know Him better.

He will begin to change you inside and out through His Word while all along the way, removing those who will hinder your walk with Him. He will leave you with a true support system via divine connections to walk with you. Most importantly, He will fill you with the Holy Spirit to give you discernment and guidance. He will use you in ways you never imagined.

"However, as it is written: 'What no eye has seen, what no ear has heard, and what no human mind has conceived,' the things of God have prepared for those who love Him."
(1 Corinthians 2:9)

That is how wonderful God is! He is a God of second, third, fourth, and fifth chances. He loves us that much! He will never forsake you or abandon you. That alone is worthy of our praise!

The void you feel will never be able to be replaced with things or people. It will only go away when you put God in your heart. Refocus, prioritize, and minimize distractions that take you away from seeking Him. Stop focusing on the wrongs and pains you have endured. Instead, focus on what those experiences have taught you and how they have grown you into a better person when you allowed them to.

Remember:

There is beauty in pain!

Salvation Today

Are you saved?

If you are not saved, you can ask God to come into your heart today. It doesn't have to be in front of a million people; neither does it have to be difficult. God knows ALL things. He knows what you are going through and even how hard your life can be. All He wants to do is share His life with you—the life He has given you—and to give you something to live and die for because to die without a purpose is to live for no reason at all!

> "But now apart from the law the righteousness of God has been made known, to which the Law and the Prophets testify. This righteousness is given through faith in Jesus Christ to all who believe. There is no difference between Jew and Gentile, for all have sinned and fall short of the glory of God, and all are justified freely by His grace through the redemption that came by Christ Jesus. God presented Christ as a sacrifice of atonement, through the shedding of His blood—to be received by faith. He did this to demonstrate His righteousness because, in His forbearance, He had left the sins committed beforehand unpunished—He did it to demonstrate His righteousness at the present time, so as to be just and the one who justifies those who have faith in Jesus."
> (Romans 3:21-26)

About the Author

LaShundra Clark-Smith is a registered nurse with the belief that healing does not begin and end on a physical level, but spiritually from within. She helps to empower women by speaking her truth through life experiences to guide women through difficult times. It is her goal to encourage and uplift women throughout the world.

LaShundra is the author of *Clarity: Beauty in Pain*, a book to encourage women that chronicles the difficult times in her life when God had to carry her through. She has been a nurse for 11 years and married for 13 while raising four children, one who has special needs. After enduring the loss of two siblings and both parents, God's purpose for her life was made clear: to help others.

In LaShundra's free time, she enjoys spending quality time with her family, writing, planning, and hosting events.

LaShundra is available for speaking engagements and events that empower women. You can reach her at:

Email: WomenWithBalance@gmail.com

Facebook: Women with Balance

Instagram: @Women with Balance

Twitter: @WomenW_Balance

On the Web: www.WomenWithBalance.org

Lashundra Smith

www.ingramcontent.com/pod-product-compliance
Lightning Source LLC
Chambersburg PA
CBHW071914110526
44591CB00011B/1672